Selecting Instructional Materials

A Guide for

K-12 Science

Committee on Developing the Capacity
to Select Effective Instructional Materials

Maxine Singer and Jan Tuomi, *Editors*

Center for Science, Mathematics,
and Engineering Education

National Research Council

National Academy Press
Washington, D.C.

NATIONAL ACADEMY PRESS • 2101 Constitution Avenue, NW • Washington, DC 20418

NOTICE: The project that is the subject of this report was approved by the Governing Board of the National Research Council, whose members are drawn from the councils of the National Academy of Sciences, the National Academy of Engineering, and the Institute of Medicine. The members of the committee responsible for the report were chosen for their special competences and with regard for appropriate balance.

The National Research Council (NRC) is the operating arm of the National Academies Complex, which includes the National Academy of Sciences, the National Academy of Engineering, and the Institute of Medicine. The National Research Council was organized in 1916 by the National Academy of Sciences to associate the broad community of science and technology with the Academy's purposes of furthering knowledge and providing impartial advice to the federal government. Functioning in accordance with general policies determined by the Academy, the Council has become the principal operating agency of both the National Academy of Sciences and the National Academy of Engineering in providing services to the government, the public, and the scientific and engineering communities. The Council is administered jointly by both Academies and the Institute of Medicine. Dr. Bruce Alberts, President of the National Academy of Sciences, and Dr. William Wulf, President of the National Academy of Engineering, are chairman and vice chairman, respectively, of the National Research Council.

The Center for Science, Mathematics, and Engineering Education (CSMEE) was established in 1995 to provide coordination of all the National Research Council's education activities and reform efforts for students at all levels, specifically those in kindergarten through twelfth grade, undergraduate institutions, school-to-work programs, and continuing education. The Center reports directly to the Governing Board of the National Research Council.

Development, publication, and dissemination of this report were supported by a grant from the Robert W. Woodruff Foundation, Inc. Any opinions, findings, or recommendations expressed in this report are those of the authors and do not necessarily reflect the views of the Robert W. Woodruff Foundation, Inc.

Library of Congress Cataloging-in-Publication Data

Center for Science, Mathematics, and Engineering Education. Committee on Developing the Capacity to Select Effective Instructional Materials.
    Selecting instructional materials : a guide for K-12 science / Committee on Developing the Capacity to Select Effective Instructional Materials, Center for Science, Mathematics, and Engineering Education, National Research Council ; Maxine Singer and Jan Tuomi, editors.
        p. cm.
Includes bibliographical references and index.
    ISBN 0-309-06533-X
    1. Science—Study and teaching—United States—Aids and devices. 2. Science—Study and teaching—Aids and devices—Purchasing—United States. I. Singer, Maxine. II. Tuomi, Jan. III. Title.
  LB1585.3 .C45 1999
  507.8—dc21

                                99-050481

Additional copies of this report are available from National Academy Press, 2101 Constitution Avenue, NW, Lock Box 285, Washington, DC 20055
Call (800) 624-6242, (202) 334-3313 (in the Washington metropolitan area)

This report is also available online at http://www.nap.edu.

Printed in the United States of America

COMMITTEE ON DEVELOPING THE CAPACITY FOR SELECTING EFFECTIVE
INSTRUCTIONAL MATERIALS

Maxine Singer, *Chair*, Member of the National Academy of Sciences and the
Institute of Medicine, President of the Carnegie Institution of Washington,
Washington, DC

Ines Cifuentes, Carnegie Academy for Science Education, Washington, DC

David Hartney, Buffalo State College, First Hand Learning, Inc., Buffalo, NY

Michael Lang, Phoenix Urban Systemic Initiative for Mathematics, Science, and
Technology, Phoenix, AZ

Carlo Parravano, Merck Institute for Science Education, Rahway, NJ

Jo Ellen Roseman, Project 2061, American Association for the Advancement of
Science, Washington, DC

Gerald Wheeler, National Science Teachers Association, Arlington, VA

Staff

Jan Tuomi, Study Director

Christine Mirzayan, NRC Intern

Doug Sprunger, Senior Project Assistant

Kathleen Johnston, Editor

Jim Lawson, Editor

Sally Stanfield, Editor, National Academy Press

Estelle Miller, Book Designer, National Academy Press

SELECTING INSTRUCTIONAL MATERIALS:
A GUIDE FOR K-12 SCIENCE

This report has been reviewed by individuals chosen for their diverse perspectives and technical expertise, in accordance with procedures approved by the NRC's Report Review Committee. The purpose of this independent review is to provide candid and critical comments that will assist the authors and the NRC in making the published report as sound as possible and to ensure that the report meets institutional standards for objectivity, evidence, and responsiveness to the study charge. The content of the review comments and draft manuscript remain confidential to protect the integrity of the deliberative process. We wish to thank the following individuals for their participation in the review of this report:

Joan Abdallah
American Association for the Advancement of Science

D. Bruce Montgomery
Mtechnology, Inc.
Massachusetts Institute of Technology

Lawrence A. Shepp
Rutgers University

Susan Sprague
Education Consultant
Mesa, AZ

Dale Stein, Emeritus
Michigan Technological University

James Trefil
George Mason University

While the individuals listed above have provided many constructive comments and suggestions, responsibility for the final content of this report rests solely with the authoring committee and the NRC.

Dedicated to the memory of Christine Mirzayan, 1970–1998,
whose curiosity, energy,
and ability to apply scientific insight to societal affairs
helped launch this project.

Preface

In 1996, the National Academies published the *National Science Education Standards (the Standards)* for grades K-12. This effort responded to a call from our nation's 50 governors who requested that standards be developed as an important step in improving science education in the United States. Since then, the National Academies have established the Center for Science, Mathematics, and Engineering Education and published reports designed to help school districts and others assure that all K-12 students achieve the level of science understanding defined by the *Standards*. Most of the states have in turn developed their own science education standards guided by the national framework.

This report by the Committee on Developing the Capacity for Selecting Effective Instructional Materials is addressed to school districts, school district administrators, individual schools, school administrators, teachers, scientists, school boards, parents, and the community at large. It provides a tested procedure for the evaluation and selection of K-12 science instructional materials that is consistent with state and/or national standards and thereby supports the learning of science by all students. The first section of the report contains background information about curricula and current selection procedures, including the review and selection efforts of other institutions. After describing its own processes, the Committee presents a "Guide to Selecting Instructional Materials," which has been designed to assist local school districts in training evaluators and carrying out an effective review and selection process.

School personnel across America are seeking concrete guidance in the difficult task of identifying instructional materials that provide opportunities for students to learn the types of science content described in the *Standards*. The variety of science instructional materials available is daunting and the quality is uneven, making the tasks of evaluation and selection challenging. But an intelligent choice is essential to achieve the important goal of improved science education for all Americans.

Acknowledgments

The National Academy of Sciences gratefully acknowledges the Robert W. Woodruff Foundation for its generous financial support of the Committee on Developing the Capacity for Selecting Effective Instructional Materials and this report. Any opinions, findings, conclusions, or recommendations expressed in this material are those of the Committee and do not necessarily reflect those of the funder.

The development of the review and selection processes and tools would not have been possible without the cooperation and assistance of state and school district science educators, who tried out various forms of the tools, allowed observations of their processes and discussions, and provided direct suggestions to the study director. Our deep appreciation to the following individuals and groups:

Herb Brunkhorst, California State University, San Bernadino, and participants in the Inland Area Science Project, University of California, Riverside;

Kathy Comfort and participants in the California Science Implementation Network;

Bob Dean, University of California San Diego, and Nancy Taylor, San Diego County Office of Education, and participants in the California Science Project, San Diego;

Terry Lashley, Director, Appalachian Rural Systemic Initiative at the University of Tennessee and participants in the initiative from Kentucky, North Carolina, Ohio, Tennessee, Virginia, and West Virginia;

Maria Lopez-Freeman and the leaders of the California Science Project sites;

Bruce McEwen, Head of the Hatch Laboratory of Neuroendocrinology at the Rockefeller University and Member of the National Academy of Sciences; Bonnie Kaiser, Director of Precollege Science Education Programs; and the New York City scientists and teachers in Rockefeller University's Science Outreach Program;

Patricia Morse, University of Washington, and Seattle and Spokane scientists and teachers participating in the review of high school texts sponsored by the American Institute of Biological Sciences and the David and Lucile Packard Foundation;

Tom Peters, Director at the Anderson Oconee Pickens Hub, and the participants from the other 12 hubs of the South Carolina Systemic Initiative for science and mathematics education; and

Lin Tucker, Melanie Barron, and teachers in the Cambridge, Massachusetts Public Schools and their scientist partners through Project Astro.

Bill Gillam, Math Specialist at the Bamberg/Calhoun/Orangeburg Math/Science Hub at South Carolina State University, pored over the cost calculation worksheet, constructed a spreadsheet, and ran real costs through it until the paper and electronic methods agreed. This is a feat many attempted and no one else accomplished.

Contents

Selecting Instructional Materials

Section I
Developing the Capacity for Selecting Effective Instructional Materials

1
The Relationship of Instructional Materials to Achieving K-12 Science Standards

The goal of the Committee on Developing the Capacity for Selecting Effective Instructional Materials ("the Committee") was to produce a tested standards-based instrument that would be helpful to people who select instructional materials for use in the science classroom. In so doing, the Committee was responding to the request of teachers for instructional materials that would enable them to teach science using a standards-based approach. Without these standards, many teachers will continue to teach science as they have in the past, and the efforts to increase student achievement will falter.

The Committee recognized early on that the selection instrument would have to be flexible in order to accommodate both national and state standards, as well as the diversity of standards and interests involved in decision making at the local level, including teachers, principals, science supervisors, parents, scientists, and school board members. Consequently, the selection instrument,

which begins on page 41 of this report as the *Guide to Selecting Instructional Materials,* has been designed for use with whatever standards have been adopted by the relevant school district.

BACKGROUND

The importance of science education has been discussed in depth in tens if not hundreds of professional and popular articles and books, including the *National Science Education Standards* (NRC, 1996) and *Benchmarks for Science Literacy* (AAAS, 1993). These discussions reflect two fundamental conclusions. First, a basic understanding of science is vital for everyone, because science and technology have become relevant to enterprises as varied as business, agriculture, manufacturing, law, and government, and they have a profound impact on many contemporary personal, social, and political issues. Second, the security and economy of the nation will depend on generating a sufficient number of well-trained scientists and engineers. Thus, science education in U.S. schools must be effective for all students, encouraging talent and interest wherever it is found (NSB, 1998, 1999).

A Nation At Risk (NCEE, 1983) challenged our country to improve science education for all students. While we have made some progress, much work remains. The Third International Mathematics and Science Study (TIMSS) showed clearly that while American elementary school students perform well in comparison to their foreign counterparts, their performance steadily declines in middle and high school (NCES, 1998a; Schmidt, McKnight, and Raizen, 1997; Schmidt and McKnight, 1998; NSB, 1998) Research associated with the TIMSS project found that many science textbooks in use in the United States emphasize breadth of coverage at the expense of deep understanding of fundamental scientific concepts (Schmidt et al., 1997; Schmidt and McKnight 1998). Even if the TIMSS data and interpretation are flawed in some respects—as some have argued (Rotberg, 1998; as referenced in Schmidt and McKnight, 1998)— we should take them as a serious challenge as we continue our efforts to improve instruction and performance.

SCIENCE EDUCATION STANDARDS

The publication of the *National Science Education Standards*, abbreviated in this report as *Standards* (NRC, 1996), represents the core initiating element in the National Academies' response to the challenge of changing and improving science education in the United States. Complementary and consistent activities are ongoing at the American Association for the Advancement of Science under the title Project 2061 (AAAS, 1989, 1993).

The *Standards* (NRC, 1996) and *Benchmarks for Science Literacy* (AAAS, 1993) were developed to provide goals for the entire nation. They implicitly recognize that U.S. educational policy is made and implemented locally in the states and school districts. It is expected that, depending on local interests and needs, diverse routes will be taken to reach the goals of the standards. Nevertheless, national standards are important if all children are to experience successful science instruction. Currently, there is enormous local variability in the quality and quantity of science programs. In 1996, for example, 41% of eighth grade students in North Dakota met or exceeded the national Goals 2000 proficiency performance standards in science, while only 5% and 20% of eighth grade students in the District of Columbia

Throughout this report the following conventions are used to address the variety of "standards" for science education: The **National Science Education Standards** are referred to as *Standards* (with a capital "S") and the **Benchmarks for Science Literacy** are referred to as *Benchmarks*. These two documents are referred to as *national standards*—both being intended to provide guidance nationally and being largely consistent with one another (AAAS, 1997). The standards developed or adopted by states, school districts, or educational enterprises such as "America's Choice" are referred to as *standards* (with a lower-case "s") or *local standards*.

and California, respectively, achieved this level (NCES, 1998b; NEGP, 1998).

Many state governments expressed support for President George Bush's 1989 initiatives to establish national goals for education and responded favorably to the *Standards* (Stedman, 1993). According to the National Science Board (NSB, 1999) and others (CCSSO, 1997; Celebuski, 1998), all states have adopted or are adopting standards for science education. While these differ extensively in content, breadth, and rigor, the adoption of standards of some kind by all states marks a significant advance. Neverthe-

less, without a continuing effort to bring state or national standards into the classroom, even those school systems poised to reform can fail to accomplish change. For example, although 66% of public school principals have stated that they require application of standards in science lessons (NEGP, 1998), data indicate that teachers rarely adhere to the standards' recommendations (NCES, 1998a). Data from earlier initiatives to improve science teaching suggest that teachers often do not receive the needed intellectual, financial, and administrative support for new initiatives (Bybee, 1996, 1997; Hutchinson and Huberman, 1993).

The development of the *Standards* took into account various factors that contribute to the ineffectiveness of current science education. These include excessively broad curricula with no time to cover topics in depth; absence of hands-on participation in science experiments; the didacticism of much science education; the absence of inquiry-based instruction; poor initial and continuing teacher education in science and science teaching; inadequate provision of necessary materials and equipment; and the poor quality of many available teaching materials, especially textbooks. Hundreds of teachers, scientists, school administrators, educational researchers, and others participated in the development, drafting, review, and final revisions of the *Standards* (NRC, 1996).

Since the publication of the *Standards*, the National Research Council has established the Center for Science, Mathematics, and Engineering Education and has published various reports designed to help school districts and others apply the *Standards* (NRC, 1997b, 1999a,b, forthcoming). The long-term goal of these activities is achieving quality science education for all K-12 students in the United States.

The *Standards* encourage teachers to engage students in the process of scientific inquiry by directing them to ask questions about the natural world, design experiments to answer these questions, interpret the experimental results, and discuss the results with their peers. Such inquiry-based teaching enhances student understanding of scientific concepts (NRC, forthcoming), and it is intended to equip all students with the analytical skills they will need in the future to interpret the world around them. Importantly, although the *Standards* stress inquiry-*based* teaching, they do not assume that all science can be learned through an inquiry process, given the amount and diversity of scientific concepts that should be learned.

Besides describing scientific content to be learned by grades 4, 8, and 12, and encouraging research-based teaching methods, the *Standards* present stan-

dards for school district administrators, principals, and policy makers, including local school boards (NRC, 1996). The document also contains guidance to help schools develop effective science education programs, specifying a need for:

- a curriculum design that presents content at each grade level that is appropriate in depth and number of topics covered for the age and previous educational experience of the students;
- teacher education and continuing professional development that support the curriculum and provide teachers with the skills needed to teach science with an inquiry-based approach;
- provision of adequate science materials to all classrooms;
- assessment methods that are consistent with the curricula and provide reliable methods for evaluation of student learning and teacher instructional proficiency;
- parental involvement in understanding the nature of good science programs and in planning improvements;
- commitment of the community, including local business, in ways that demonstrate the relevance of science to adult life and work; and
- recognition by local and state school administrators and boards of the vital importance of an understanding of science and technology for the future success of children.

Some of these elements have been further addressed in detailed reports by the National Research Council and others (Bybee, 1996, 1997; NRC, 1997a,b).

Finally, for science teaching programs to achieve the goals of the *Standards,* teachers and students will require access to instructional materials that are accurate in science content, clear in their presentation of scientific concepts and processes, appropriate for the age of the children who will use them, and suitable for the local community, as well as consistent with the aims of the *Standards.* This report deals with this issue.

INSTRUCTIONAL MATERIALS

Instructional materials for K-12 school science include textbooks, laboratory manuals, other books about scientific matters, kits, software, CDs, and other multimedia materials, such as videos, that provide equipment and materials for specific inquiry-based lessons. Not only are these materials a primary source of classroom science learning, but because the professional development for teachers is often structured around instructional materials, they also play a profound role in the education of teachers. Thus, to achieve the learning goals of the *Standards* or *Benchmarks,* students and teachers

must be provided with instructional materials that reflect these standards. Moreover, teachers will be more likely to provide the requisite classroom experiences if professional development programs provided by school systems are grounded in standards-based instructional materials. For these reasons, the selection of instructional materials that reflect the learning goals of the standards is a central issue. This is no simple task, since schools and school districts must select from among the broad array of materials produced by U.S. publishers. As documented in the TIMSS project, many instructional materials used for teaching science in the United States emphasize breadth of coverage at the expense of a deep understanding of fundamental scientific concepts (Schmidt et al., 1997).

Ultimately, teachers decide what to teach in the classroom, and many teachers—especially elementary school teachers—base their lesson plans on the class textbook and on other instructional materials rather than on the "intended" curriculum specified by official policies (Woodward and Elliot, 1990). In 1991, Horizon Research, Inc, surveyed 930 past winners of the Presidential Award for Excellence in Mathematics and Science Teaching (PAEMST), comparing them with a random national sample of 2,065 elementary math and science teachers.

PAEMST teachers rely far less than their peers do on textbooks in their teaching. Only 17% of presidential award-winning science teachers of grades 1-6 said they consider textbooks a "major influence" on what they teach. By contrast, 59% of the national sample of science teachers overall felt that way (Weiss, 1991). Thus, instructional materials play an unexpectedly important role in education: when the materials align with the standards, teachers are more likely to attend to the standard's goals; when they align poorly, teacher goals will diverge from those of the standards.

Another important effect on what teachers teach arises from assessment practices. Statewide assessments can dictate much of what teachers teach. Not surprisingly, teachers want instructional materials that can help them prepare students for mandated assessments. "Assessment of student performance exerts extraordinary influence on the lives of children and their families and on every level of the education system" (Stern, 1999), including the selection of instructional materials. The approaches to science education in the *Standards* stress classroom assessment as a critical component of instruction. Such assessments are needed by the teacher in order to identify what the students have learned and not learned,

thereby informing the subsequent instructional topics and processes. However, statewide assessments generally have a different purpose. They are designed to measure what a student has learned at a given point in time. Moreover, the dependence of the tests on a multiple-choice format tends to put a premium on memorized and isolated facts in comparison to understanding of science concepts. For example, in a 1994 study of assessments in 17 states that test science achievement, only 7 states' assessments were found to include items designed to measure conceptual understanding and application, and 15 of the state tests primarily focused on basic skills measured by multiple choice items (CPRE, 1996). Teachers, principals, school district administrators, and parents may question whether instructional materials that are aligned with standards will enable students to do well on the statewide assessments.

In addition, instructional materials affect teaching indirectly by influencing the greater community. For instance, parents use the content of the student materials or textbooks to examine what their children are learning. Often the sole link to the classroom, these materials can determine whether parents support or object to the school science programs.

Procedures for Selecting Instructional Materials in Public Schools

There is a great deal of variation from state to state with respect to the statutes, policies, regulations, and resources governing local K-12 education and the selection of instructional materials. Some states mandate that state adoption guides, recommended lists, or state standards be considered; and political issues sometimes affect the development and enforcement of state policies. Ultimately, however, the local level is where the final decisions are made about which science instructional materials will make it into the classroom.

According to information gathered by the Council of Chief State School Officers, 13 states specify that the state will determine which instructional materials may be used or that the state will publish a list of materials from which local school districts may choose. In another 8 states, state authorities recommend materials, but the selection is actually carried out by the local districts. In all of these states but one (Idaho, where districts are restricted by law and must choose only state-approved materials), districts can choose other materials by following a waiver process (CCSSO, 1997). In California, for example, a school district can seek approval from the state board of education to spend state instructional material allocations on materials not on the state adoption list (IMF, 1989).

State adoption lists influence the education of many U.S. students; the adoption list in California alone represents 10% of the textbook market nationwide, or 5.6 million public school students (CBEDS, 1997). Consequently, adoption or recommendation is, for publishers of instructional materials, a high-stakes make-or-break business that provides access to large markets. This is especially true in the largest adoption states—California, Texas, and Florida—which together represent 20% of the national textbook market (Wheeler, 1999b).

Competition for adoption or recommendation causes publishers to adopt cost-saving measures by publishing a single textbook that is acceptable in several states (Tyson, 1997). To do so, textbook publishers often sacrifice quality for quantity by covering multiple curricula (many of which are broad to begin with), thereby sacrificing depth for breadth (Tyson, 1997). As outlined in *A Splintered Vision: An Investigation of U.S. Science and Mathematics Education* (Schmidt et al., 1997), such materials tend to emphasize scientific vocabulary at the expense of the acquisition of fundamental understanding of scientific concepts.

State and local selection procedures for instructional materials may require vendors to make formal presentations and provide multiple samples of their wares, as well as professional development for teachers if the materials are chosen. Small vendors often lack the resources to provide such services and are therefore virtually excluded from consideration. However, small suppliers may offer quality science instructional materials. The effect of these practices is to limit the availability of materials that could substantially contribute to attaining the learning goals.

Common Considerations in the Local Selection of Science Instructional Materials

In the 29 states where there are no state-level policies for selection or recommendation of instructional materials, the challenge of finding appropriate instructional materials falls entirely on individual districts or schools. Local school districts may receive some assistance from the state educational authorities. The amount and kind of support, which varies from state to state, may include technical support from state science supervisors or state science consultants, who bring varying degrees of science content expertise to the selection. In comparison to state selection committees, the district or individual school selection committees may be less familiar with standards, and they often lack sufficient human and financial resources for establishing a

well-informed and thorough selection procedure.

In these 29 states, publishers play a lesser role. Those charged with making selections can make use of various publications that describe and, in some cases, evaluate instructional materials. Among these are the guides published by the National Science Resources Center (NSRC, 1996, 1998), Project 2061 (Roseman, Kesidou, and Stern, 1997; Roseman, 1997a,b; Kesidou, 1999; AAAS, forthcoming a,b,c); and the National Science Foundation (NSF, 1997).

Just as there is great variation across states regarding the policies and practices for selecting science instructional materials, each local context is different in terms of culture, capacity, and process. Nevertheless, there are several issues that arise repeatedly during local decision making:

- What is the budget for the review and selection process?
- From whom can the committee obtain current information about expenditures for such items as instructional materials and professional development?
- What student performance and enrollment data are currently available? From whom can the committee get additional data?
- Does the district have in place the facilities and systems to support a standards-based science program?

- Who will be responsible for facilitating the instructional materials review and selection process?
- Who will comprise the review and selection committee(s)? How will they be chosen?
- How will the review and selection committee members be prepared for their task?
- How will the review and selection committee(s) function? How will decisions be made? How and by whom will the final recommendations be made?
- What will be the role of district administrators? What degree of influence will district personnel have on the selection process?
- How will a list of vendors be generated?
- What materials and information will be solicited from the vendors?
- What other sources of information will be provided to the committee(s)?
- What are the district's standards or learning goals? Are they widely accepted and in use?
- Are the current instructional materials aligned to the standards? Are they being used?

Procedures for Selecting Instructional Materials in Private Schools

In the United States there are a variety of schools other than those administered by local public school systems; these include parochial schools, independent schools, nationally administered public schools run by for-profit organizations (e.g., the Edison Project Schools), and a growing number of public charter schools. Informal inquiries have revealed selection procedures that range from school-wide coherent policies, to departmental committees, to selection by individual teachers.

The Edison Project, for example, selects materials centrally and the same materials are used in all its schools (currently 24,000 students in 50 schools in 12 states). The selection process is initiated by setting curriculum standards and objectives with the advice of consulting groups. Their science standards are described as a synthesis of the *Standards* and *Benchmarks*. Instructional materials are then evaluated with reference to the standards. Among the issues considered are (1) how well the materials will support the teachers and (2) evidence that the materials (or program) actually works. The Edison Project reports that there are insufficient studies on science learning to help very much with evaluation of efficacy (Chubb, 1999).

An urban, independent elementary school that emphasizes its science program reported that a science department committee first defines the curriculum and then selects texts or kits that dovetail with the curriculum. It is generally assumed that a single text or multigrade program will not be adequate; rather, a main text and supplementary materials are chosen. Additional considerations include (James, 1999):

- Will the materials support the scope and sequence of the curriculum?
- Do the materials consider the history of the scientific discipline?
- Are supplementary readings provided at multiple reading levels so that both advanced and learning-disabled students can find appropriate readings?
- Are meaningful projects and investigations embedded in the text?

An urban, independent high school reports that departments and teachers have a great deal of independence in instructional material selection. The teacher who will use the materials makes the final decision. The first step is to consider the topics to be covered. This is based on a prior departmental consideration of *Standards* and *Benchmarks* and definition of the skills to be acquired before graduation. Then materials—generally textbooks—are inspected for their match to the topics. Materials for inspection are obtained from publishers and also by visiting a local university's education library. Additional considerations include:

- Does the text make it possible for the teacher to choose the order in which topics are presented?
- Is the material clearly written?
- Are laboratory exercises included in the book itself?
- How challenging is the material?

Selected materials are presented to other teachers in the department for inspection and comments before the teacher decides on a textbook (McArthur Parker, 1999).

Common Issues Arising During Selection

When selecting science instructional materials, certain problematic situations are common, examples of which are described below.

- Publishers typically claim that their science instructional materials are standards-based. Because this may not always be true, evaluators need to establish the reliability of such claims (Kesidou, 1999).
- There are vastly different pedagogical approaches in science instructional materials. Some materials are designed around an inquiry-style pedagogy; some emphasize hands-on materials; and others are textbooks that may or may not offer materials for student investigations. Failure to

distinguish among these approaches risks the selection of materials inconsistent with district requirements. Yet, even experienced teachers may not perceive the goals of the standards when they occur in innovative materials (Bush et al., forthcoming).

- Selection committees may choose materials without recognizing that their effective classroom use depends on providing teachers with extensive professional development in the pedagogical approach embodied in the materials. Such a situation arises, for example, if the materials represent an activity-based or inquiry-based science program, and the teachers have traditionally depended on textbooks and didactic lessons (Little, 1993).
- A related issue is the influence of assessments. Assessment tools used in the school district need to be consistent with the learning goals, pedagogical approach, and assessments built into the materials (Webb, 1997).
- Financial resources are almost always an issue. The amounts budgeted for instructional materials may not be sufficient to purchase desirable materials, and tradeoffs may be required. Budget restrictions may also result in the use of dated, even inaccurate, materials long after they should have been set aside.

INSTRUCTIONAL MATERIALS AND TEACHING

Instructional materials are a primary source of science learning in the nation's classrooms. In high schools and middle schools, textbooks are essential supplements to the limited amount of material that can reasonably be presented in the classroom time available to the teacher. Packaged instruments and materials (kits) for laboratory and hands-on experiences are an enormous help to busy teachers at all levels, K-12. The availability of excellent instructional materials is critical for elementary school teachers who, in spite of minimal formal scientific education of their own, are called on to teach a range of scientific concepts from chemistry to natural history, earth science, astronomy, and ecology. The closer instructional materials adhere to the goals of state and national standards, the more likely the teacher is to succeed in achieving those goals.

The Influence of Instructional Materials on Professional Development

Instructional materials influence the continuing professional development of teachers in several ways. For elementary school teachers, the materials often provide basic information on content and pedagogy. Formal professional development for teaching the curriculum may be provided, but it is often brief and superficial—especially with respect to the content standards (Massell, Kirst, and Hoppe, 1997). Instructional materials are often accompanied by teacher manuals, which are important resources for teachers. If the goal is to teach according to standards, the quality of the instructional materials is as important to teachers as it is to students.

Because instructional materials influence curricula, they also affect the content of professional development workshops covering the adopted curriculum; in particular, inexperienced teachers who are preoccupied with the practicalities of teaching are interested in workshops directly related to their lesson plans (Loucks-Horsley, Stiles, and Hewson, 1996). Thus, the quality of the instructional materials will directly affect the quality of the teaching.

The review of instructional materials during a selection process, if well structured, can serve as an important professional development experience for participants. Review processes that require understanding of the standards and foster rigorous analysis of the materials can be powerful learning experiences (Brearton and Shuttleworth, 1999). Teachers engaged in such reviews can develop a better understanding of the science content, the requirements for inquiry-based teach-

ing, and the resources needed for standards-based science instruction.

THE CRITICAL IMPORTANCE OF INSTRUCTIONAL MATERIALS

In the United States instructional materials direct class curriculum and instruction, define the accuracy of the science knowledge imparted, influence professional development of teachers, and affect the educational roles of parents. From the perspective of promoting standards-based science education, instructional materials are critical tools. Adoption of materials that promote the learning of important ideas and skills is then essential if standards-based education is to become a reality in the nation's classrooms. Such materials would improve curricula and significantly impact daily teaching practices (Tyson, 1997; Tyson-Bernstein, 1988).

Current selection procedures, particularly those at the local level, often lack the capacity to sift systematically through instructional materials and identify those that align with the adopted standards. Evaluation procedures are needed to encourage evaluators to become knowledgeable about the standards and use them when judging instructional materials. Such evaluation procedures would, ideally, also be educational experiences for the evaluators. Teachers and local school boards can, with the assistance of knowledgeable scientists, ultimately build the capacity to judge the materials themselves. The task becomes more formidable as the number and variety of materials increases in traditional textbook form, in packaged lessons such as kits and videos, and now on the Internet. At present, the conditions surrounding materials selection may lead evaluators to review materials superficially and choose those that look attractive, appear to reduce budget outlays, or simplify teachers' roles. For this reason, building the local capacity to select instructional materials that support the goals of state and national standards is of paramount importance.

2
A Review of National Efforts to Evaluate Instructional Materials

Acknowledging the diversity of ways schools select instructional materials and the variety of national, state, and local standards, the Committee sought to design a practical and flexible evaluation approach that can be useful across the nation.

The Committee began its work by examining related national efforts and familiarizing itself with the nature of the task and relevant issues. The Committee then established a set of key principles to guide the development of an evaluation tool. This chapter of the report describes these aspects of the Committee's work. Chapter 3 "The Development of a Guide for Evaluating Instructional Materials" describes the adopted principles and the process the Committee used to develop and test an evaluation tool. The tool itself is presented in Chapter 4 as the "Guide to Selecting Instructional Materials."

The Committee studied several national efforts to provide states and localities with guidance in the review

and selection of K-12 science instructional materials. These efforts are summarized below. Chapter 5, Contact Information, and the references provide information on how to access these tools.

PROJECT 2061

The American Association for the Advancement of Science, through its Project 2061, has developed a tool for evaluating how well instructional materials are likely to contribute to the attainment of specific learning goals in science, mathematics, and technology (Roseman et al., 1997; Roseman, 1997a,b). Working closely with scientists, mathematicians, educators, and curriculum developers, the project staff formulated and tested a procedure for analyzing curriculum materials that attends to both content alignment with standards and instructional design. Experience with this tool indicates that it provides consistent results from one reviewer to another (Kulm and Grier, 1998). The procedure

(1) uses research-based criteria;
(2) requires extensive training (four days are recommended to train evaluators to minimum competency);
(3) demands evidence-based arguments to support all judgments; and
(4) involves two review teams in the examination of each material and subsequent reconciliation of differences.

The procedure can be applied to a variety of K-12 materials, ranging from those that cover a few weeks to several years of classroom programs (Roseman et al., 1997; Roseman, 1997a,b). Although the procedure has been developed for use with the learning goals in *Benchmarks* (AAAS, 1993) and the *Standards* (NRC, 1996), it is applicable to state or district curriculum frameworks if the learning goals are clearly articulated.

Project 2061 used a four-step evaluation process: identification of learning goals, content analysis, instructional analysis, and summary report (AAAS, forthcoming c). The process clustered its evaluation questions on content analysis into three groups:

(1) accuracy (examined by scientists and to be published in *Science Books and Films*);

(2) alignment with standards; and
(3) coherence.

Material found to be aligned with standards is then subjected to the instructional analysis to determine the likelihood of students learning the specific benchmarks and standards that serve as a basis for the analysis. The seven clusters of evaluation questions (each benchmark-specific) on instructional analysis are:

(1) providing a sense of purpose;
(2) taking account of student ideas;
(3) engaging students with phenomena;
(4) developing and using scientific ideas;
(5) promoting student thinking about phenomena, experiences, and knowledge;
(6) assessing progress; and
(7) enhancing the learning environment.

Also see "Instructional Analysis" in Chapter 5.

Project 2061 has applied its analysis procedure to middle school science textbooks and will publish a report titled *Middle Grades Science Textbooks: A Benchmarks-based Evaluation* in fall of 1999 (AAAS, forthcoming b). A report on the evaluation of middle grades mathematics programs has also been published and is available on the Project 2061 website (See Contact Information).

THE NATIONAL SCIENCE RESOURCES CENTER

The National Science Resources Center (NSRC), co-sponsored by the National Academy of Sciences and the Smithsonian Institution, collects and disseminates information about exemplary teaching resources; develops and disseminates curriculum materials; and sponsors outreach activities in the form of leadership development and technical assistance to help school districts develop and sustain hands-on science programs.

In 1988, the NSRC published its first compilation of critically reviewed elementary school curriculum materials for teaching science (NSRC, 1988). This was updated in 1996 with the publication of *Resources for Teaching Elementary School Science* (NSRC, 1996). In the latter volume, the materials include core instructional materials, supplementary materials (such as activity-centered units) and activity books, as well as the *Science and Technology for Children* instructional materials produced by the NSRC itself. According to the preface, these materials were reviewed for their consonance with principles advocated in the *Standards*, particularly those that "emphasize student inquiry, teaching for understanding, and the inclusion of science as a core subject in every grade level,

starting in kindergarten." Information on obtaining the NSRC evaluation tool used for the review is available in "Contact Information" at the end of the book.

The NSRC has released an additional volume *Resources for Teaching Middle School Science* (NSRC, 1998)). The preface states that all the curriculum materials listed are "standards-based," that is, a panel of teachers and scientists found them to meet the NSRC's evaluation criteria for middle school science curriculum materials (NSRC, 1998).

THE NATIONAL SCIENCE FOUNDATION'S FRAMEWORK FOR REVIEW

For many years, the National Science Foundation (NSF) has supported the development of instructional materials for K-12 science education. The NSF's goal has been to develop high-quality materials that have potential for national impact. In 1996 the NSF developed and implemented its Framework for Review to help it answer two questions: (1) What are the characteristics of the portfolio of comprehensive instructional materials for middle school science developed with NSF funds? and (2) How sufficiently do these materials provide for a comprehensive program for middle school science consistent with national standards? The study and its results were published, and information on obtaining the report and Review Framework (NSF, 1997) is available online.

The NSF designed its review framework as a peer review exercise for use by NSF evaluation panels composed of scientists, science and technology educators, and science teachers. It requires written responses as well as an overall numerical rating on a five-point scale. Because no materials were evaluated by more than one panel during the NSF evaluation, no conclusions can be drawn about the reliability of the instrument or the process.

The framework is designed to review recent NSF-supported middle school curriculum materials that contain a year or more of course materials. Major criteria to be addressed by framework users are:

- Is the science content correct?
- How well do the materials provide for conceptual growth in science?
- How well do the materials align with the *Standards*?

Notably, the NSF framework addresses only briefly the question of whether the materials under review are likely to lead to student learning and understanding. It does ask whether the materials provide guidance to teachers, suggestions for appropriate instructional strategies, ideas for a variety of assessment activities, suggestions for implementation, and whether they accommodate student diversity.

THE U.S. DEPARTMENT OF EDUCATION

The U.S. Department of Education (DoEd) established an expert panel in 1996 to develop a process for identifying promising and exemplary programs (including instructional materials) in science and mathematics. The panel established criteria and trained teams of reviewers to evaluate instructional materials that publishers voluntarily submitted. The criteria were:

(1) The program's learning goals are challenging, clear, and appropriate for the intended student population.
(2) The program's content is aligned with its learning goals and is accurate and appropriate for the intended student population.
(3) The program's instructional design is appropriate, engaging, and motivating for the intended student population.
(4) The program's assessment system is appropriate and designed to provide accurate information about student learning and to guide teachers' instructional decisions.

(5) The program can be successfully implemented, adopted, or adapted in multiple educational settings.

(6) The program's learning goals reflect the vision promoted in national standards in science education.

(7) The program addresses important individual and societal needs.

(8) The program's assessment system helps teachers select or modify activities to meet learning needs.

The detailed criteria are available on the DoEd's website and can be used by state or local review teams for evaluation guidance (DoEd, 1997c). The DoEd plans to publish lists of programs that meet its criteria at the promising or exemplary levels. The designation of exemplary will require evidence of effectiveness and success.

CENTER FOR SCIENCE, MATHEMATICS, AND ENGINEERING EDUCATION

The National Research Council's Center for Science, Mathematics, and Engineering Education (CMSEE) has published other reports that encourage the thoughtful selection of instructional materials aligned with standards. CMSEE's Committee on Science Education K-12 and the Mathematical Sciences Education Board will jointly publish

Designing Mathematics or Science Curriculum Programs: A Guide for Using Mathematics and Science Education Standards (NRC, 1999a). As stated in that report, its purpose "is to assist those who are responsible for making decisions about curriculum with the process of improving the coherence of mathematics and science curriculum programs." The report focuses on ways states and local school districts can develop, or adopt and transform standards into a logical, grade-by-grade curriculum. It recognizes that one aspect of curriculum development must be the selection of appropriate instructional materials, materials that can support the grade-by-grade goals for student learning according to the pedagogical approaches embodied in the curriculum. Moreover, it emphasizes that the process of developing a curriculum program must be flexible while it considers the interplay between the curriculum itself and the instructional materials available to support the curriculum. Such flexibility is required to assure coherence throughout K-12 instruction, while limiting the need for individual states or school districts to undertake the challenging and costly job of developing new instructional materials to match its chosen curriculum program. The report discusses some general guidelines for the work of selecting instructional materials and emphasizes the need to assure scientific validity and alignment with content and pedagogical standards. It then refers to instruments available for structuring the tasks, including instruments under development (such as the one presented in this report) or already published (as summarized above).

In 1998 the National Academy of Sciences published *Teaching About Evolution and the Nature of Science*, which includes a section on the evaluation of instructional materials with respect to the inclusion and alignment of material on evolution.

3
The Development of a Guide for Evaluating Instructional Materials

This chapter documents the general principles and rationale for the Committee's decisions and describes the process used to develop an evaluation tool and a guide for the tool's use. The process was designed as an investigation that began with a review of the evaluation tools developed by others (see Chapter 2). The Committee then established a set of working principles to use in designing its prototype evaluation tool. Potential users field tested the prototype to provide information to guide the Committee in making revisions. The chart below outlines the process.

Developmental Milestones	Desired Results
Examine existing review tools.	Determine need for and attributes of a tool for school district use.
Practice using various tools.	Create a common base of review experience.
Establish general principles.	Develop basis for designing the tool.
Design a prototype review tool.	Implement desirable attributes identified to date.
Use the prototype to review the materials to be used in first field tests.	Test prototype usability and generate review data to compare to field test results.
Field test at three sites, keeping type of participants, tool, directions, and quality of facilitation as constant as possible.	Gather information to be used in revising the tool.

(continued)

Developmental Milestones	Desired Results
Revise the tool and draft a guide of sequential steps and recommended processes.	Determine what information and resources would be most helpful to facilitators of the review, selection, and approval processes.
Field test at three sites with diverse needs and participants, varying the training approaches.	Gather data to be used in revising the guide and revise the tool as needed.
Conduct two focus groups.	Complete both the tool and the guide.

THE COMMITTEE'S PRELIMINARY REVIEW OF MATERIALS

The Committee reviewed a selection of science instructional materials in order to reach consensus on the challenges of developing a tool for evaluation and establish a framework for discourse. This exercise provided the context for designing early versions of the evaluation tool for use in initial field tests. The varied professional experiences of the Committee members (science teachers, scientists, science supervisors, and science curriculum designers) provided a rich mix of ideas. The discussion focused on the best way to obtain data on what students would learn in a classroom where the teacher uses the instructional material in question.

Committee members examined a range of life sciences materials. They discussed how to focus reviewer attention on the alignment of the material with content standards and on how well the material would support student learning of that content. For example, simply checking off whether a particular standard is "covered" does not provide useful information for making judgments about the likelihood of students learning the science content embodied in that standard. Judging the quality of the instructional design needs to be tied to the question of what students are likely to learn if the particular materials are used. It became clear that to obtain informative evaluations, reviewers also must first identify the set of science education standards for which the instructional material is to be examined and then evaluate it standard by standard. In addition, it would be important to obtain information on the extent of professional development required to achieve effective teaching with the materials and the cost of this teacher education process.

The Next Step: Designing a Prototype Evaluation Tool

After its study of current selection practices, an investigation of other efforts to develop evaluation tools, and some practical experience in carrying out evaluations, the Committee designed its process for developing and testing an evaluation tool. It formulated a shared set of principles on which the tool would be based, including a goal of fulfilling needs not met by other organizations' efforts. The Committee then constructed a prototype tool and subjected it to an iterative process that cycled experiences from field tests and focus groups back to the Committee to inform the modifications made in subsequent drafts.

GENERAL PRINCIPLES

The Committee established the following general principles as the basis for its design of a prototype evaluation tool.

1. The evaluation tool should fulfill needs not met by other instruments. The Committee identified unmet needs from its analysis of the review tools available for instructional materials. We found, for example, that the National Science Foundation's (NSF) Framework for Review is designed for materials that cover pro-

grams of a year or more of classroom work, and that it addresses only briefly the question of whether the materials under review are likely to lead to student learning and understanding (NSF, 1997). The latter question was therefore selected for emphasis in our prototype tool. The National Science Resources Center's (NSRC) *Evaluation Criteria for Science Curriculum Materials* (NSRC, 1998) does not ask reviewers to evaluate materials against specific *Standards* or *Benchmarks*, which the Committee deems necessary. The Project 2061 review tools require highly trained evaluators and weeks of effort (Roseman et al., 1997), and they are not feasible for many local school districts with limited time, funds, and expertise. Moreover, none of these tools articulate a process that encompasses both evaluation and selection processes.

2. The evaluation tool should assume that a set of standards and a curriculum program or framework will inform the work of evaluators in appraising the effectiveness of instructional materials. Evaluation of science instructional materials is a formidable task. A set of standards and a curriculum program or framework documents the school district's expectations for science education and serves as an important reference for the evaluation. Moreover, the existence of such policies implies an established community support for the science education program, which in turn can promote acceptance of recommended instructional materials.

Since education in the United States is controlled at the local level, in many instances evaluators will need to use their local or state standards rather than the *Standards* or *Benchmarks*. The Committee at first considered producing a tool that encouraged selection of material aligned with national standards. However, it realized that a tool that is applicable to local standards would be more widely used and would foster the understanding of standards and encourage their use. The Committee therefore resolved to make a flexible tool that could be used with any standards and in many situations including the review of a whole instructional program, a series of units, or individual units of instruction.

3. An evaluation process should require reviewers to provide evidence to support their judgments about the potential of the instructional materials to result in student learning. Other review tools designed for use in limited time periods commonly use a checklist of items for consideration, a numerical scale, and weighted averages of the numerical evaluations. Use of such tools can result in a superficial evaluation of a set of materials that may identify the content standards

covered, but fail to indicate whether the coverage will help teachers foster student learning and understanding. The Committee concluded that a rigorous evaluation process must continually challenge reviewers to identify evidence of the materials' potential effectiveness for this important purpose.

4. Evaluators will more likely provide critical and well-thought-out judgments if they are asked to make a narrative response to evaluation questions or criteria, rather than make selections on a checklist. When asked to construct a narrative response, an evaluator has to develop a cogent and supportable statement. This requires more careful thought than simply checking items on a list. By their very nature, narrative responses help build understanding on the part of an evaluator and can, therefore, serve as professional development. In addition, narrative responses give evaluators more latitude to assess materials in the context of local goals and needs and allow the evaluators (teachers and scientists alike) to contribute their own knowledge and experience to the task. The Committee concluded that the tool should require evaluators to provide their professional judgment as narrative responses and thereby encourage a critical analysis of the materials.

5. An effective evaluation process must include one or more scientists

on the review teams. Published science instructional materials are not always scientifically sound or up to date. Moreover, some materials do not consistently reflect an understanding of what is and what is not important in a particular scientific discipline. The Committee found, in its examination of instructional materials, many cases where materials contained detailed information of little relevance, extensive unnecessary vocabulary, and only cursory treatment of the essential concepts. Scientists on the review team are helpful in judging the accuracy of the science presented in the material and the importance of the information for understanding essential concepts.

6. **An evaluation instrument needs to serve diverse communities, each one of which has its own needs.** Since an evaluation instrument for instructional materials will be used by different groups for a variety of purposes, no single model can be assumed. In most cases, school district evaluation groups will use it; however, individual schools and statewide evalua-tion groups will also use the tool. These evaluation groups will have varying resources, and the students being taught will differ with respect to language proficiencies, economic status, abilities and disabilities, and home support resources. Therefore, the Committee resolved to design a tool that is adaptable.

7. **Tension exists between the need for well-informed, in-depth analyses of instructional materials and the real limitations of time and other resources.** The National Sci-ence Teachers Association surveyed some 10% of its members just before the release of the *Standards,* in January 1996, to ascertain their perceptions of the barriers to implementation of these national standards (Wheeler, 1999a). Two major impediments were identified: lack of time and lack of other resources. The Committee resolved to develop a tool that recognizes the real limitations faced by the evaluators of instructional materials.

8. **Many evaluators (including teachers, administrators, parents, and scientists) using the tool will be unfamiliar with current research on learning.** Curriculum decisions are not always informed by research on learning, but rather on what feels comfortable to teachers, what seems to work, or what is expected (Orpwood, 1998). Once teachers have completed their formal education and begun to teach in the classroom, access to research publications and the time to review them are a challenge. Most scientists also lack the time and interest to delve deeply into education research. In addition, the typical professional development workshops for teachers rarely devote time to in-depth study of

current research on learning (Loucks-Horsley et al, 1996). Therefore, the evaluation coordinator should be strongly encouraged to provide references and resources for research on learning, including the *Standards* (NRC, 1996), *Benchmarks* (AAAS, 1993), and more recent studies (NRC, 1999a,b).

9. It is more important to evaluate materials in depth against a few relevant standards than superficially against all standards. The pressures of limited time and funds can drive an evaluation team to inspect instructional materials superficially against all relevant standards. The Committee concluded that if time and funds are limited, it is preferable for the team to select a small number of high-priority standards for an in-depth examination.

10. The review and selection processes should be closely connected even when reviewers are not members of the selection committee. In some school districts, one team evaluates instructional materials and reports to another group that is responsible for final approval and selection. In others, one team is responsible for both evaluating and selecting instructional materials. Considerations such as cost, the local district's ability to refurbish materials, and political acceptability (e.g., attitudes about teaching evolution) may play a role in the final selections.

The Committee concluded that in all instances it is important that final selections be based primarily on a standards-based review. It is therefore important that one or more of the members of the evaluation team be on the selection committee.

PROTOTYPE TOOL AND FIRST ROUND OF FIELD TESTS

The Committee's initial prototype tool was designed to include the following characteristics:
- reliance on the professional judgment of reviewers;
- substantiation of review ratings by cited evidence;
- ability to be completed in a reasonable amount of time;
- focus on the extent to which the instructional materials matched a standard; and
- consideration of scientific inquiry as content and as a way of teaching and learning.

The Committee members tested the prototype themselves. To begin, they participated in a preliminary review of sample materials and compared their results with one another. After scanning materials on middle school environmental science from seven publishers, they chose three that represented various types for closer review. One was an eight-week kit-based unit, another was a section from a textbook, and the third was chosen because the Committee agreed that it was likely to get a low rating because of inadequate and inaccurate content coverage and an absence of attention to scientific inquiry. Each Committee member used the first draft of the prototype tool to review one of these instructional materials. The results were useful in giving each member the experience of trying a standards-based review and a context with which to assess the results of the field tests.

First Round of Field Tests

The goal of the first field test was to investigate the levels of expertise of typical reviewers and their reactions to the prototype tool. The prototype tool was used by three sets of teachers and program administrators interested in instructional materials review. Each set reviewed the same middle school environmental science materials considered by the Committee. One test involved leaders from four states cooperating in a rural systemic initiative supported by the NSF. The second test included members of a statewide professional development program for science. The third test was conducted by school district leaders in a state-led science education program. The tests took place in different parts of the country.

No training was provided for any of these field tests and the Committee's facilitator (the study director), who conducted the test, did not coach the reviewers. The reviewers used standards of their choice, and both local and national standards were used.

In general, the reviews from the field were less critical than those of the Committee members. In particular, the materials that were included in the field test sample because of their obvious inadequacies were deemed mediocre, rather than poor or unacceptable. The Committee members had registered concern about the lack of attention to scientific inquiry in the reviewed textbook, but inquiry was largely ignored in the field reviews. In almost half of the field reviews, it was unclear whether the reviewer had used a standard as the basis for the review in spite of written instructions to do so. Thus, the reviewers seemed to misunderstand the main focus of the review tool. When a reviewer failed to cite standards, it was unclear whether the reason was frustration with the tool, a lack of knowledge of the standards, or some other reason.

Some reviews were insightful while others were shallow. The most perceptive were produced by those individuals with a high level of classroom experience and a deep knowledge of standards.

The quality of evidence presented by reviewers to back up their judgments was very uneven. The Committee members had not included much prompting or structure in the prototype tool, in the hope that the field reviewers would apply their personal expertise to construct compelling evidence-based arguments.

Most of the field reviewers made positive comments about their participation in the review. They indicated that they considered the process to be a professional growth experience and showed by their hard work and attention that they found the endeavor worthwhile. A more detailed analysis of the results of the first field test and the Committee's follow-up decisions about the next draft of the tool are summarized below.

Committee's Analysis of and Response to the First Round of Field Tests

1. The time needed to review one unit of instructional materials with the prototype tool was about 3-4 hours. Reviewers indicated that the time requirement was too long to meet their needs at the district level in a realistic way.

   Committee's response: Further streamlining of the review tool.

2. Many reviewers did not base their review on one or more standards, in spite of explicit instructions to do so.

   Committee's response: Revision of the format and editing to make the use of standards unavoidable. Introduce training as a preliminary to the use of the tool.

3. All three sets of reviewers rejected a review criterion that required publishers to supply data on the materials' effectiveness based on field tests or other research findings. They considered the criterion unlikely to produce useful information.

   Committee's response: The Committee decided to eliminate this criterion in the interest of keeping the process as streamlined as possible. However, this decision was not made easily, since the Committee members were also interested in emphasizing that evidence of effectiveness should be required of the developers and publishers of instructional materials.

4. The ratings did not strongly match those predicted by the Committee. The field reviewers were more likely to identify strengths than weaknesses. They recorded recommendations that

were uncritical and unlikely to be of much help in sorting and selecting from a number of choices.

Committee's response: Clarify the criteria and add specific recommendations for reviewer training.

5. The degree to which the instructional materials involved students in scientific inquiry did not appear to be an important criterion for the reviewers, although it is an essential standard in the *Standards*.

   Committee's response: Strengthen this important criterion and add recommendations for reviewer training.

6. Consideration of the cost of the materials, an element in the prototype tool, seemed to confuse reviewers, required extensive research, and did not contribute to the evaluation.

   Committee's response: This consideration was moved to a new selection phase of the tool. It was not deleted because it will be an important final consideration.

7. In one of the three field-test groups, most of the reviewers had previous experience in instructional materials

review and strongly suggested the use of a rubric for each criterion. In the education profession a rubric is a scale that includes a detailed definition of each rating level for each criterion.

Committee's response: Refrain from recommending the use of rubrics in order to remain flexible in meeting local needs and to encourage and honor the individual judgments of reviewers.

8. The experiences with all three review groups indicated that training of the evaluators would be required in order to assure a reference to standards as an integral part of the process, to include the consideration of inquiry-based learning as an important feature of instructional materials, and to encourage the exercise of individual, independent judgment.

   Committee's response: Prepare a training guide to accompany the tool.

9. The field test exposed the separate procedures used for evaluation and selection in some school districts. The prototype tool blurred the different considerations and people involved in these two processes.

Committee's response: Redesign the tool so that evaluation and selection can be carried out by either the same group or two different groups.

10. Discussions with the field-test groups revealed that although there had been considerable work by others to develop evaluation tools for science instructional materials, no one had undertaken the task of guiding states and districts for the purpose of carrying out a standards-based selection process for these materials.

Committee's response: Include in the training guide advice on organizing and carrying out evaluation and selection, designed for the school district facilitators of these processes.

SECOND ROUND OF FIELD TESTS USING THE MODIFIED TOOL

The Committee modified the prototype tool according to the elements listed above and added a guide that included the requisite training for reviewers. The modified tool was used in a second round of field tests. This included discussion meetings and review activities at three new sites, described below. During this round of field tests, the groups could choose the materials to be reviewed and the Committee's facilitator (the study director) experimented with training methods. Therefore, each field test in this round had unique features. This testing provided an opportunity to learn more about how the tool could be used in a variety of situations, allowed an evaluation of the addition of training to the procedure, and informed subsequent revisions to the guide.

Site One

The first test site of the second round was based on a one-day meeting of four groups, each consisting of two teachers and two scientists. A district science coordinator convened the groups to consider whether an elementary science unit currently in use in the district was aligned with state science education standards. The teachers in the group had taught the unit and were therefore familiar with the materials. The scientists also knew the materials because they had assisted the teachers one-on-one in understanding the materials and using them in the classroom.

The reviewers spent much of the time discussing the standards that they had been assigned to consider. All four groups emphasized that the standards against which the materials were to be judged were overly broad. Three of the four groups completed a review of the materials under consideration, but the time available was insufficient to thoroughly document reviewer work.

Site Two

At the second test site, a State Systemic Initiative coordinator brought together some 30 reviewers (including science and math educators, scientists, and mathematicians) from across the state for a day and a half to learn how to review and select science and math instructional materials.

Before beginning the review, the facilitator began the review training by discussing examples of review comments that cited evidence either effectively or ineffectively. Subsequently the reviewers were asked to generate their own definitions for the review criteria specified by the tool. This took nearly two hours to reach consensus.

The reviewers then divided into 8 groups and, using 18 standards, conducted a mock review of one middle school science unit that was in use in a number of school districts in the state. Because the unit did not meet the two content standards, several reviewers expressed concern that the standards-based review would undermine the use of the unit that had been chosen by their school district. Expressing satisfaction with the process as a whole, the reviewers said they viewed the process as one they could use to select instructional materials, despite concerns about the time involved.

Site Three

At this site, a group of nine research scientists and four teachers reviewed a popular advanced placement biology textbook. The outreach director of a university program served as facilitator. No reviewer training was provided. The standards, review documents, and instructional materials were mailed to each participant in advance of the meeting. Each reviewer was instructed to spend no more than five hours reviewing the high school text.

The group discussion revealed some confusion about the task purpose. One reviewer asked, "Are we reviewing the materials, the instrument, or the standard"? Over half of the submitted review forms did not mention the standard used. Interestingly, all the scientists judged the materials as having completely met the standards, while all the teachers stated that the materials met the standards incompletely.

Committee's Response to the Second Round of Field Tests

As a result of the second round of field tests, the guide was modified and amplified as described in the following paragraphs. Experience with the diverse review situations in which the tool was used suggested that the guide should include straightforward practical advice regarding its use.

The guide was modified to make the references to standards more prominent and more frequent. For example, Form 1 directs reviewers and the facilitator to identify standards that should be top priority. Form 2 requires the full text of the standard to be entered. These simple processes help ensure that a reviewer attends to the standards when documenting a review. Furthermore, the summary judgment of the reviewer must be expressed as an opinion about the extent to which students are likely to achieve the standard. Toward the same end, each step of the suggested review process reiterates the overall goal of increasing student achievement by applying the standards.

Scientists participated at each site during the second round of field testing, in each case contributing a point of view that complemented that of the educators and emphasizing their importance to a thorough evaluation. The most significant contribution of scientists is attention to the accuracy, completeness, and presentation of the content. Participating scientists described their experiences as valuable and enlightening.

The second round of field testing demonstrated that reviewer training can improve the quality of the review by providing more extensive and convincing evidence. For example, at one site

the reviewers, before beginning their own process, were shown examples of poor responses, then better responses, and then very good responses. The examples used are included in Chapter 5 "Resources for Training." Training also proved useful in defining the review criteria. Reviewers at one site found that generating definitions of each of the criteria as a group was useful, and the group's reviews were more comprehensive than those of any other field test. A sample agenda for generating these definitions is found in Chapter 5 "Resources for Training."

The training and review process described in the guide is as streamlined as possible and will require *at least* two days of training, followed by one hour of deliberation and writing for each standard used. Nevertheless, every field test produced some participant objections about the length of the process. The Committee is satisfied that the process presented here has been designed with this concern in mind and cannot be shortened without sacrificing the intent and validity of the review process. The Committee hopes that experience with a standards-based review will convince both the reviewers and the teachers and students who use the materials that a careful review is worth the time invested. Local facilitators of this process are encouraged to develop creative strategies to join forces and share both resources and results to lessen the individual costs for a thorough review.

It is realistic to expect that the guide can be used successfully in a variety of circumstances. The review process described in the guide contains recommendations that have been constructed to highlight only the principles and main tasks of each step. Specifics are left to the professional judgment of the facilitator and reviewers, because nearly every situation will have unique features. Suggestions for some specific situations have been included in "Constraints and Cautions" sections in Chapter 4.

LESSONS LEARNED

The development process described in detail above provided Committee members with experiences and evidence concerning the need for a new kind of review instrument and the impact of myriad local concerns. A summary of the lessons learned may be useful in developing the capacity of the science education community to recognize and use effective instructional materials.

Training is essential if the evaluations are to be valid and useful. Field tests were carried out both with and without prior training. The sophistication and depth of the evaluations carried out

after training were significantly improved compared to those obtained when training was omitted. In part this is because the tool asks the evaluators to exercise independent judgment without the guidance of detailed questions and check-off boxes for responses. This approach was not familiar to most evaluators, and they therefore benefited from training, including a group 'mock' evaluation, before they began their work. The requirement to exercise independent judgment and provide a narrative explaining the evidence for the judgment was challenging to participants in the field trials. Frequently, there was a request for more specific questions and accompanying boxes for checking off responses. The Committee responded positively to a few of these requests in subsequent versions of the tool, however the Committee concluded that the challenge to evaluators in the final tool is a useful one for fostering understanding of standards and for developing the capacity to carry out thoughtful evaluations.

As already noted, many teachers are unfamiliar with pertinent modern learning research. Training sessions need to include explication of the most significant aspects of this research. This can be accomplished by reference to the *Standards* and *Benchmarks*, supplemented by more recent work, such as *How People Learn* (NRC, 1999b).

The field trials demonstrated that many evaluation team members are not sufficiently familiar with the applicable standards to carry out the review tasks without training. Moreover, some members of evaluation teams are not inclined to refer consistently to the standards, preferring to make judgments based on their own views of what should be included in the instructional materials. Training must therefore include a description of the applicable standards, the way they were developed, and why it is important to base evaluations on the standards. The goal of this training is to assure that all evaluators accept the applicable standards as the basis for their judgments.

Another lesson learned from the field trials concerns the priorities given to different aspects of the review materials. In the absence of training, some reviewers made no priorities among the several criteria being considered. There was, in some instances, resistance to the idea that the quality of the scientific content and pedagogical approach must take priority over all other criteria (e.g., quality of pictures and diagrams, teacher aids, cost, or applicability to a bilingual school setting). In such cases, the relative quality of the materials became secondary. Apparently, current practice does not always give precedence to these two critical matters.

Participants in the field trials consis-tently found that the time required to complete the review was too long. This was true even though the Committee was attentive to this issue in the earliest version of the tool, and at each iteration attempted to streamline the process. It was common for the review of an individual material to take between two and four hours, even when both the pertinent grade level and relevant standards were restricted. In an actual evaluation process, for example, six different materials might be under consideration, requiring between 12 and 24 hours of work. To this, the time required for training and for follow-up discussions by the evaluation team must be added. Subsequently, evaluation of another set of materials may be re-quired for a different grade level or a different set of standards. The total time required is a difficult assignment for classroom teachers and working scientists, except perhaps when the task is carried out during vacation time. In that case, compensation should be provided (Tyson-Bernstein, 1988). This is a serious issue because a thorough, thoughtful review with reference to standards is, by its nature, a lengthy process. The Committee considered some strategies to help ameliorate this problem. The most promising strategies included limiting the review materials to materials judged acceptable by the NSRC (NSRC, 1996, 1998) or Project

2061 (AAAS, forthcoming a,b,c); setting aside materials that are plainly inadequate; or selecting a limited number of materials to be reviewed based on information acquired from other states or school districts. However, any such narrowing of the field to be reviewed should be employed with caution. Considering the magnitude of the instructional materials investment and the societal costs of failure to educate students successfully, adequate resources —including time— to accomplish the selection of the best possible instructional materials must be provided. Developing the capacity of the reviewers and paying attention to local standards for student learning are responsibilites that are too important to be evaded.

The field-test teams' comments underscore the diversity of opinion, experience, goals, and standards that exist in the 50 states and the thousands of school systems. Moreover, comments and reactions to the tool were different depending on where in the K-12 years the instructional materials were designed to be used.

OBSERVATIONS

This report should be considered a beginning. The Center for Science, Mathematics, and Engineering Educa-tion plans to continue the work begun by this Committee by disseminating this report and encouraging its use. It is expected that wide application will reveal additional desirable modifications to the guide and tool. The Committee envisions that the tool will be regularly revised in response to experience and ongoing learning research.

The Committee recognized an inherent difficulty in trying to determine whether a particular instructional material is "good." The definition of "good" must include an assessment of the match between the instructional material and the applicable standards, learning goals, and pedagogical approaches. The critical question is whether the material will increase the likelihood that students will attain the knowledge defined by the standards and goals. That is, will the material be effective? Here the Committee found itself on uncertain ground, and evaluation teams will have similar experiences. There is no adequate body of research on this topic. There is, of course, a literature that evaluates pedagogical approaches and what children are capable of learning and understanding at different ages (NRC, 1999b). But on the question of the specific attributes of effective materials, little is known.

Conventional analysis of teaching effectiveness is based primarily on student performance on standardized tests. As already described, such tests often fail to adequately assess understanding of scientific concepts and knowledge about specific aspects of the natural world (CPRE, 1996). Moreover, most assessments evaluate the effectiveness of a student's entire learning experience; they do not distinguish between what students learn from instructional materials and the teaching centered on the materials, as distinct from what they have learned from their own activities and experiences and from their parents. There is no substantial body of research that tries to evaluate the effectiveness of particular instructional materials as a separate variable in the total learning experience. The one reasonably well-documented example of such a study evaluates a sixth grade unit on "Matter and Molecules" (Lee, Eichinger, Anderson, Berkheimer, and Blakeslee, 1993). In the absence of a substantial body of research, the use of tools such as the one described in this report will depend to some extent on the experiences that evaluators bring to the review and selection processes. Classroom experience, while informative, cannot, for many reasons, be considered definitive or unbiased. The Committee urges that extensive research on the effectiveness of instructional materials be promoted in the near future.

Section II
Recommended Processes and Tools

4
Guide to Selecting Instructional Materials

INTRODUCTION TO THE GUIDE

The instructional materials used in K-12 science classes provide the basis for what students can learn and what teachers should teach. The process used to select those materials is critical to providing students and teachers with a solid foundation for achievement and successful teaching. This guide is designed to help school personnel review and select science instructional materials. Specifically, this guide will be most useful to anyone appointed to facilitate the process—for example, a district or state science program administrator, a science department head, or a school principal. The facilitator will work with both the review and selection teams and eventually will seek approval from a school board, advisory board, or principal.

In some cases, individual schools or teachers may work alone to review and select materials; in other cases, communities and states may review and recommend materials for adoption lists. Since the applicable policies and logistical arrangements are highly variable, this guide cannot address all situations. Rather, the guide is based on principles and processes that individuals, committees, and communities may adapt for their unique circumstances and needs.

The review process is designed to be more open-ended than most and to rely heavily on the professional judgments of the reviewers rather than scales, formulas, and averages. As such, it is similar to the type of review used by scientists to evaluate each other's scientific work. This may be perceived to be a drawback because this type of review will be new to most reviewers of instructional materials. In addition, in order to produce a reliable review, reviewers will need to be versed in the standards, to have experience teaching the grade levels for which materials are being considered, and to have the knowledge and understanding of science as described in national standards. In the end, the experience of carrying out the kind of rigorous review that is common in the scientific world, requiring so much background, will be valuable on many levels. It will provide a significant professional growth experience for many reviewers, help develop a local capacity to select and implement a strong science program successfully, and contribute to developing leadership among local science educators.

Assumptions

This guide and the process it advocates are based on four key assumptions:

1. The selection of instructional materials can be carried out either for a comprehensive science program or for a small part of such a program. The process in this guide can be used equally well for a variety of selection needs: selecting materials for a multiyear program (for example, K-5, 6-8, or 9-12); meeting a specific goal (such as identifying instructional materials for a new ninth grade physics course); or selecting a single unit of study for part of a year.

2. The review of instructional materials, which precedes selection, will be based on standards; that is, specific student learning goals. Applying standards to the process makes student learning of important concepts and skills a key factor in making

selection decisions. It is also assumed that local policies will determine the source of the standards to be used—national, state, or local.

3. A curriculum framework (see box) is in place that is based on standards and describes a scope and sequence for student learning. It also is assumed that the selection process involves decisions about which instructional materials are most likely to help students achieve the learning goals given in the framework.

4. At least two people will review each instructional material, and a group including both experienced teachers and scientists will collaborate in the review process. Experienced teachers contribute their knowledge of how children learn, how to manage a classroom learning environment, and the particular challenges of the local

> "Curriculum framework," as used here, means the design for a science program. Frameworks can be official documents representing a mandate approved at the state, county, or district level or can be working documents, useful for sketching out proposed components of a multigrade science program. Many frameworks are published as a matrix of topics and grades or grade ranges. A review and selection process can identify resources for each cell in the matrix.

student population. Scientists can contribute their broad knowledge of science content and scientific inquiry and can be particularly helpful in reviewing the importance of the content and its accuracy.

Review and Selection Process Overview

The review and selection process in this guide differs from some other processes in that it has been designed to rely on the individual and collective judgments of the reviewers, not on checklists, scales, or rubrics. The judgments are based on standards, and incorporate evidence about how likely it is that students will learn through use of the materials. The final products include a review team summary report and recommendations to the decision-making body. Provision is made for consideration of the costs of the materials and reviewer opinions about the need for teacher professional development. These processes are designed to be flexible to suit various purposes, timelines, and available resources.

The review process generates information about the quality of instruction units—the building blocks of a complete science curriculum. The selection of a collection of materials should not be viewed as the equivalent of constructing a multiyear curriculum program. For more information about constructing a complete science program, see *Designs for Science Literacy* (AAAS, forthcoming a) and *Designing Mathematics or Science Curriculum Programs: A Guide for Using Mathematics and Science Education Standards* (NRC, 1999a).

The review and selection process presented here is written as a guide for the person responsible for organizing and carrying out the task, the facilitator. The complete process is made up of five steps:

1. A Facilitator Plans the Review.
2. Training Reviewers.
3. Carrying Out the Review of Materials.
4. Selecting Materials.
5. Evaluating the Process and Results.

There are consequences for omitting any of the parts, some of which are discussed in sections entitled "Constraints and Cautions." If, over time, the entire process is implemented, and increasing numbers of teachers and community members have an opportunity to participate, the local capacity to select effective instructional materials will be greatly enhanced.

STEP 1: A FACILITATOR PLANS THE REVIEW

As the facilitator, you should begin planning at least a year before final instructional material selections are scheduled to be made. During this planning time, you will be gathering data about the effectiveness of existing science education programs, becoming familiar or reacquainted with state and local policies concerning instructional materials selection, and constructing an action plan and budget. In the process, you will be contacting school personnel and community members for information and opinions, as well as building awareness of the existing program and the possible need for changes.

Recommended Process

Policy information. Compliance with policy is necessary to gain final administrative approval and access to funds for new instructional materials. For example, you will need to know whether your state produces lists of materials from which you must select materials and when state and local funds will become available. Information about deadlines can be especially important in budget planning and for avoiding unnecessary delays. Find out how flexible the policies and regulations are and the consequences of not conforming to policy. Take advantage of the Internet, conferences, and publications to stay current.

If your local plans and needs conflict with state policies or regulations, you have time to build administrative and community support for solutions. Find out about policy waivers and the recent history of how many have been granted. Talk to local administrators about the options available and your concerns in order to gauge their support. Make sure you know the history of local selection practices.

Budget planning. Each review situation will have unique policies and resources for completing the review. At a minimum, develop a budget for two days of training prior to the actual review—one to understand the process and define the criteria and one to do a mock review. In order to make a rough estimate of the time that will be required to do the review, use the following guideline taken from field-test experience: three hours per reviewer (use a minimum of two reviewers) to carry out a review using three standards on one piece of instructional material that is designed to support about eight weeks of the school curriculum.

These minimal time recommendations assume that:

• some community scientists are already informed of and involved in science curriculum planning, implementation, and evaluation, and therefore are comfortable working with school personnel;

- your potential reviewers have a reasonably deep understanding of standards; and
- professional development for science teachers and ongoing community outreach has developed a broad common understanding of effective science education programs and practices.

If the preceding capabilities are not available, you will need more resources for as many capacity-building activities as possible.

Be sure that you have provided funds for the staff required for the extensive preparation and facilitation of the review and selection processes. Also plan for the time and associated costs required for community outreach activities. Obtaining and organizing the materials to be reviewed can be very time consuming. Your budget should adequately allow for this task and any shipping or storage fees that may be necessary.

Coordination with other science education initiatives. Contact those persons responsible for curriculum and instruction inside and outside your immediate program. Use their advice to compile a broad account of local science education efforts, including a history of

recent professional development in science, sources of current funding, and projects and programs in science teaching and learning that are under way or planned. Research new science education initiatives being discussed or to be launched soon in the region or state. Coordination with the plans and proposals of others involved in science education in your area may enable you to share resources for recruiting and training reviewers, developing community support for the science program, and planning for the successful implementation of the new program. Become familiar with the processes used and lessons learned by colleagues in other disciplines who have recently completed instructional materials selection. Make a written summary of these findings. These will be useful later in training reviewers and making presentations to administrators and community groups.

Data collection. Compile and analyze evidence on current student achievement in science, teacher opinions on what is working, elements of the science program in need of revision, and community perceptions of the science program. An anonymous survey of the materials that teachers are actually using may be necessary, since the curriculum prescribed by current policies may not be the one that has been implemented in the classroom. A survey of parents and students will not only collect useful data, but also increase interest in the review, selection, and approval processes.

In addition to the basic reporting of standardized test scores, a study of the item analyses can provide useful data on student achievement. This information is usually provided along with the overall scores to school administrators. Professional development in how to interpret and apply the test-item analysis information is useful for principals and teachers, who are then better prepared to provide information on student achievement. In regions that disaggregate the test scores in a number of ways—by gender, race, courses, or classrooms—it is possible to further pinpoint needs that should be taken into consideration in selecting instructional materials.

Another source of data related to student science achievement is enrollment data in upper-level science courses, in which students enroll by choice or by meeting prerequisites. Improvements in the science courses should show a trend to increased demand and enrollment for advanced courses, as well as an increased participation of currently underrepresented minorities.

The information collected before the review will help influence final selection decisions and provide compelling background information in support of your recommendations during the approval process.

Identification and involvement of community stakeholders. Support from influential members of the community will be critical when recommendations for the ultimate selections need to be approved and when the new materials are introduced into schools. Selected local scientists and engineers from industry, faculty of local colleges and universities from both the education and science departments, and leaders of science education programs can be made members of an advisory board, along with teachers, students, and parents. Some members of this board may become reviewers and trainers. Participation in the advisory board and in the review and selection process will help educate community members about the curriculum, standards, classroom needs, and available instructional materials.

Involve the community in learning about the science program through district, school-level, and community activities such as open house events, community meetings, and newsletters. Educate participants about program goals and the science standards and gather opinions and suggestions. Keep community members informed through periodic updates using all of the news media available in your community.

Recruit reviewers. Choose highly qualified people whose judgments can be trusted to help increase student achievement in science. Selection criteria should include science content knowledge, demonstrated knowledge of effective teaching practices, and depth of knowledge of science standards. Individuals who have participated in professional development in science will have a common base of experience. Recruitment will be enhanced by including a description of the training to be provided and the professional growth benefits of participation.

Science subject matter knowledge is the most fundamental requirement for reviewers. Teachers often will have acquired this knowledge through classes and experience outside the district's professional development program. Therefore, be sure to collect background information on all potential reviewers, including their college majors, previous experience, and summer internships, through an application process.

To identify a pool of potential teacher reviewers, obtain information on participants in past professional development for science teachers. This may also be a useful exercise for identifying scientists and university faculty who could serve as reviewers. Community advisory groups and partnership activities may also yield potential reviewers, such as practicing scientists and engineers. By all means, try to identify those who have had experience working with school personnel. Consider requesting information from each potential reviewer on possible conflicts of interest and sources of bias, such as participation in professional development sponsored by publishers, past and present consultant agreements, or experience in publisher field tests. Reviewers need not necessarily be excluded because of these activities: when the team convenes, possible biases and conflicts of interest should be declared by each individual and that information then used to avoid potential problems.

Build the capacity of the reviewers. The success of your review and selection process depends on the depth of knowledge of the reviewers—of science subject matter, standards, and effective science teaching. Invest as much as possible in building this knowledge and experience. These professional growth opportunities need not be limited to the reviewers. Wider participation will not only build capacity to review new materials but, more broadly, to accept and implement them.

Resources outside your immediate locale can help you build the necessary capacity. Various organizations provide leadership development opportunities, many focused on improving science and mathematics education. For example, Project 2061 offers extensive training in the review of instructional materials, which makes for excellent facilitator preparation even when not possible for all reviewers. National or state organizations may offer professional development on the *Standards*, *Benchmarks*, and state standards. Universities may offer seminars on how children learn and the efficacy of various assessment strategies. Partnership programs with local science and technology organizations can provide important information on current scientific knowledge and practices.

Pilot-test materials. If there is sufficient lead time (at least six months), plan to have reviewers and others actually use materials in their classrooms. This is particularly valuable when innovative instructional strategies are represented in the materials or when the materials use new technology. Provide training and support for the use of the materials to help ensure that the pilot is a fair test of the quality of the instructional materials. Initially, pilot teachers will be strongly biased by their experiences—good or bad—with the new instructional materials. Sufficient time and frequent opportunities to discuss their experiences with others can moderate the effects of this bias on the review and selection processes.

Constraints and Cautions

If you are short on time, use the policy information and science program effectiveness data that you have on hand. Depend on existing and experienced advisory bodies and educators who are interested in science. Because short timelines are unlikely to produce much of a change from the status quo, consider seeking approval for a postponement of the deadline, if necessary.

If you are short on money, give existing advisory boards preparation tasks or at least seek their help in finding resources. If policy will allow, consider confining the scope of the instructional material review to those areas identified as most in need of improvement.

If you cannot recruit reviewers according to the criteria suggested here, plan to spend more time in training the reviewers. Sometimes members of the review and selection team are political appointees, a situation helpful in gaining eventual approval of the instructional materials recommended. Adequate training will be even more important in developing a common understanding of the task and a common background knowledge about science program goals, if the members of your team have an uneven knowledge about science education standards, effective instruction, and local policies.

If the community lacks knowledge about your science program, consider who is most likely to affect the selection process and then target your outreach efforts to them. If your community has contradictory ideas about the need for science program improvement, do not skimp on this initial step of preparation. A well-planned and well-executed review process ultimately can be annulled by lack of community support. Schedule frequent progress discussions with other administrators to obtain their advice and commitment as well.

If you arrange for publisher representatives to make presentations to reviewers, try to provide a level playing field for large and small publishers. Give all presenters a common format to follow and forbid the offering or accepting of gifts (which is usually prohibited by local policy anyway). Remember that reviewers can be inappropriately influenced by these presentations, even if they involve only an overview of the program and its components. Caution reviewers to look for evidence to support the claims made by the publishers.

To save time and money, a common impulse is to narrow the field of materials to be reviewed by some kind of prescreening. Various scenarios were examined during the development of this guide, and each carries some risk of undermining a valid review process. The most promising current resources for prescreening are those reviews of science materials published by organiza-tions that have made a large investment in developing both detailed review criteria and the reviewer expertise. Most notably, Project 2061 is producing in-depth reviews based on its *Benchmarks for Science Literacy* (AAAS, forthcoming c). These reviews compare materials according to various criteria and are available on the Internet (See Chapter 5 "Resources for Training"). The National Science Resources Center has produced two books of recommended instructional resources, one for elementary school science, and one for middle school science (NSRC, 1996, 1998). The criteria used are provided as appendixes in both books, with the full text available on the Internet (See Chapter 5 "Resources for Training"). Another source of middle school science review information is the Ohio Systemic Initiative (Ohio Systemic Initiative, 1998).

If there is community-wide agreement on the success of some elements of the current science program (e.g., high student achievement and teacher satisfaction), it may be possible to keep those elements in place and focus the review on revising only those parts of the curriculum to be changed.

A publisher's claims of standards addressed or recommended grade levels should be viewed with suspicion. Only a careful review will reveal the degree to which the content of standards is actually addressed in instructional materials, or how flexible the recommended grade level may be.

Do not reject too quickly instructional materials packages without certain accessories (e.g., bilingual resources and kits of hands-on materials). Instructional materials with a great deal to offer can be too easily discarded in this way. The most appropriate time to compare such support materials is during the subsequent selection process.

STEP 2: TRAINING REVIEWERS

The training of reviewers is an essential step. The goals include developing an understanding of the purpose of the reviews, establishing a common understanding of the role of standards in the review, and fully defining the key terms and criteria to be used in the review. Mock reviews provide the necessary practice, allowing the process outlined in this guide to be adjusted to reflect local needs and values.

The training of the reviewers can also serve to broaden the experiences and background knowledge of the participants, enabling them to envision science education as it could be in local schools, not only as it is. Reviewers should be exposed to recent research in science education content and pedagogy, as well as to outstanding science education programs elsewhere in the nation.

The training process recommended here has been developed through iterative field-test processes. Although the elements have been carefully selected to be those critical for producing a successful review, the facilitator may need to adapt them to meet local needs. Sample agendas, examples, and resources are provided in Chapter 5 "Resources for Training."

Recommended Process

Develop a common understanding of review purpose. The purpose of the review process is improved student science achievement in the near future. The more detail reviewers can bring to their reviews, the more they will be able to make the best choice of instructional materials to meet local needs. In order to provide relevant detail, reviewers will need to develop a common understanding of their work.

First, members of the review team should analyze all the data gathered in Step 1. They should not only discuss the data collected about the effectiveness of the current science education program but also decide on strategies to remedy shortcomings and reinforce strengths. Reviewers should also become familiar with local policies governing the curriculum selection process and reach consensus on any choices that may be open to them about how to proceed.

Develop a depth of knowledge about standards. Each reviewer needs to become familiar with the relevant science content standards (Roseman, 1997a). If the standards document has an overview, that may be a good place to begin. Most standards documents have informative text that precedes the standards, which can provide background information, references to research, and examples of the standards in action.

Be sure that each reviewer understands which part of the main text of the document contains the standards to be used in the review. If your standards are not numbered, a system for referring to an individual standard should be developed (See "Numbering Standards" in Chapter 5).

This may be the first local review to be based on standards or the first experience that individual reviewers have had in applying standards. Reviewers should understand that standards are student learning goals and that the review must determine how likely students are to meet those goals using the instructional materials that will be under review.

Materials do not teach by themselves; so reviewers will need to judge how successfully local teachers will be in using the materials to help students meet learning goals. Reviewers should base their judgments on the explicit guidance and support the materials provide for the teacher—the teacher's guide, lab manual, directions for each lesson, overall format and organization—as well as on the availability of professional development. The reviewers are encouraged to make comments about the knowledge and experience of local teachers in the "Summary Judgment" and "Additional Information" sections of their reviews. The comments recorded for the materials eventually selected will be very helpful to those

who plan the professional development that will be required to help the teachers use new materials effectively.

Most instructional material units address more than one content standard, and some will address a standard only partially. The purpose of the review is to evaluate materials against the two to five standards of highest priority. Later, during the selection process, decisions will be made on how best to put together a sequence of instructional materials that meet all student learning goals.

Incorporate the use of selected reference materials. During training activities, introduce reference materials and model their use. The *Standards* (NRC, 1996) are especially helpful in describing inquiry, providing a broad description of each subject area at K-4, 5-8, and 9-12 grades and outlining good science teaching practices. In *Benchmarks* (AAAS, 1993) the chapter format enables a reviewer easily to survey a content area from kindergarten through grade 12. Either *Standards* or *Benchmarks* should be used to supplement local content standards, particularly when the local standards are lists of topics rather than descriptive of what students should understand. In addition, for some content areas, the *Benchmarks* chapter on the research base is a convenient reference on children's ideas and recommended teaching strategies.

Information and reference materials obtained from recent professional development in pedagogical or management areas may be helpful. For example, it may be desirable to consider the compatibility of the reviewed science instructional materials with recommended strategies for planning lessons, using cooperative groups, planning an integrated curriculum, developing language skills in content areas, or addressing the needs of bilingual and special education students.

Information about the mathematics curriculum may be necessary to help reviewers determine whether students' knowledge of mathematics is likely to be consistent with demands of particular science instructional materials.

Introduce the review forms. "Directions for Reviewers" is part of Step 3, and all review forms can be found at the end of this chapter. Form 1 is used to record the standards used for reviewing a specific instructional material, as well as the final rating for how the materials address each standard. Forms 2 and 3 include the six criteria that comprise the review—two on science subject matter, and four on student learning or pedagogy, and are to be filled out for each standard. Form 4 asks the reviewer to provide a summary rating. Form 5 records information from the reviewers on which components offered by the publisher they believe are necessary and the professional development needed to support the use of the materials. (See Figure 1 for an overview of the review process.)

All forms can be found at the end of this chapter. If you wish to customize the review forms just described, an electronic version can be copied from the National Academy Press website (<http://www.nap.edu>). It may be especially important to add to or otherwise revise the directions to include specifics about local meetings, process details, or resources.

Define criteria for student learning. The four student learning criteria in Form 3 of the review tool—active engagement (3.1), depth of understanding (3.2), scientific inquiry (3.3), and assessments (3.4)—must be discussed and described by all reviewers. During field tests of the process provided in this guide, group-generated definitions of these terms produced better and faster reviews than the use of prescribed definitions. A recommended process for generating these definitions is provided in Chapter 5 "Resources for Training."

Record, reproduce, and distribute reviewer-generated definitions of criteria produced during this part of the training. Plan to attach these to each review tool packet for reviewer use during the mock review (see below).

Provide examples of how to cite

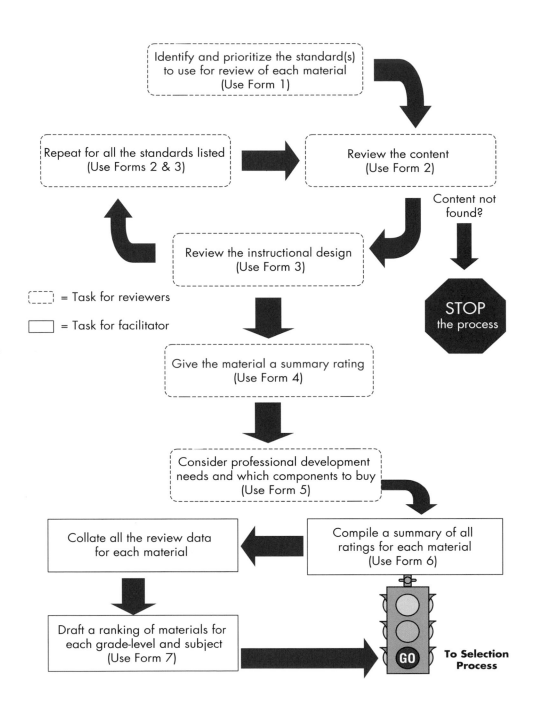

FIGURE 1   Review Process

GUIDE TO SELECTING INSTRUCTIONAL MATERIALS

evidence. The review forms ask reviewers to provide evidence, including examples, explanations, and references, to back up their judgments. Clear and complete citations will be vital to the selection process. Examples of good and poor evidence help reviewers understand what is meant (See "Citing Evidence" in Chapter 5).

Practice by doing a mock review. Practice is essential before beginning the actual review. Without it, the first review will become the training experience. For the mock review, choose a sample of high-quality instructional materials of sufficient complexity to simulate actual review challenges. For example, this could be a four- to eight-week module that contains a teacher's guide, student materials, assessments, and optional supplements.

Provide copies of Forms 1-5 of the review forms and "Directions to Reviewers." Depending on your schedule, you can answer any questions the reviewers have on the entire process before they begin their mock review, or you can proceed to answer questions one step at a time.

Have reviewers discuss their results after each section. To resolve concerns, refer back to the worksheets, such as "Definitions of Criteria" and "Directions to Reviewers," and to reference materials. Some calibration of the review process is desirable, and the discussion will be quite helpful to the reviewers. However, complete agreement on how to apply the criteria is not desirable. Diverse individual reviews, guided by the standards and backed up with evidence, will produce the most comprehensive, useful results.

Plan for reflection and evaluation of the process. Convene the reviewers at the end of the process to discuss its benefits and drawbacks and how to improve the process. Sometimes the review participants do not participate in the selection process that follows. If this is so, provide them with information about the future uses of their reviews.

Constraints and Cautions

If training for this process is minimal (for reasons of time or budget, or both, for example), reviewers will be likely to produce widely varying reviews and recommendations, and the result will be a prolonged and possibly confusing selection process.

If your standards document is sketchy, the reviewers may not have sufficient information to understand exactly what students are supposed to know or do to meet the standards. This will make review results highly variable. In some cases, the official assessments used in the region provide more information about what students should know or be able to do. But using assessments as a substitute for standards is risky. The content addressed in assessments is usually quite narrow, and the content or form of the tests may change with little or no notice. If needed and feasible, make a group decision to supplement your standards with the appropriate sections of the *Standards* or *Benchmarks*.

Be alert to the possibility that, while reviewing, reviewers may encounter unfamiliar formats and pedagogical styles. This may cause reviewers to dismiss innovative materials that could be effective (Bush et al., forthcoming).

STEP 3: CARRYING OUT THE REVIEW OF MATERIALS

In Step 3, reviewers identify applicable standards and analyze each potential unit of instructional materials to determine whether the learning goals will be met. The judgments of experienced teachers, informed and focused by training for the process, will be used. The judgments of scientists concerning the accuracy and significance of content and approaches to scientific inquiry—likewise informed and focused by training—will also be harnessed.

You may want to invite others, including school board members and district administrators, to observe the first review session. Doing so will help these key stakeholders become aware of the magnitude of the review task, the qualifications of the reviewers, and the focus on student learning goals. This knowledge will help later on, when these same individuals will be involved in making final decisions, and will help them educate the community about the integrity of the process.

Recommended Process

Make decisions about materials needed, reviewer assignments, and time needed. In assigning materials to reviewer teams, take into account the time required. For planning purposes, estimate that a review of a set of instructional materials covering about eight weeks, against two or three standards, will take at least six hours (when there are two independent reviewers). See also "Budget Planning" in Step 1.

Comprehensive instructional materials packages, such as a yearlong seventh grade science program, will require multiple reviewers. First, decide which standards must be met by the instructional materials and, if feasible, prioritize the standards. Assign each team of two independent reviewers one or two of these standards, which they will then apply in a review of the entire program. This approach ensures that the content coverage and accuracy are given priority. Their review of the student learning criteria should then be carried out for the sections in which their assigned content is found. A conference among all the reviewers is likely to be needed to address overall concerns, such as identification of any gaps, recommended components, and likely needs for professional development. The Review Team Summary (Form 4) will need to be extended to include more standards. In addition, if the reviewers engage in a wide-ranging discussion about the program, it would be helpful to attach a written summary to Form 4.

Each reviewer should be provided with at least the teacher's manual and the assessment materials. For other components, such as materials kits, videotapes, supplementary materials, and student books (if student books are reproduced in the teacher's manual), one set per team may be adequate. When videotapes or other media materials are an integral part of instruction, make the appropriate playback equipment readily available. If materials include software, CD-ROMs, or probeware, it is advisable to have a technical troubleshooter available.

Be sure to communicate to reviewers your arrangements with the publishers, which usually require that the samples be returned promptly in resalable condition.

If you have provided for adequate release time and space, the reviewers will be able to come to a central site to do the reviews. This way, the complete set of materials can be made readily available, but, more importantly, the reviewers will be available to one another. If the reviewers will be working independently off site, plan to facilitate communications with you and with each other. When the reviewers are finished with their individual reviews, you may want to schedule time for a conference among the reviewers of one set of materials. Each reviewer has made independent decisions, but defending those decisions to others and listening to other opinions may strengthen the review process. If there is a broad

range of ratings, reviewers should not be pressured to change their original rating unless they find they truly over-looked or misunderstood something. Alternatively, you can convene a conference only when the reviews indicate a need. Looking back on the quality and sources of evidence cited to support an overall judgment should reveal why the reviews differ and will provide discussion points for a conference. In some cases, it may be necessary to carry out another independent review because of disagreements.

Decide who will identify the standards to be used for each unit of instructional materials. This can be done either by you or by the reviewers. If done by you, the review will get off to a faster start. However, this standards selection is a very time-consuming task requiring reading of many materials. Each pair of reviewers assigned a small number of instructional materials can also accomplish the identification and prioritization of standards themselves. Even though it can be a disorienting experience, this approach actually produces more autonomous, flexible reviewers who appear to understand the framework, standards, and their task better. Allow plenty of time and a flexible schedule for this task. (Also see "Directions for Reviewers" below.)

Revisit the purpose and steps of

the review. During training, you discussed purpose and walked through a mock review. Now you may want to create a flow chart of all the steps in a review to help keep reviewers oriented. (Also see Figures 1 and 2.) It is not uncommon for reviewers to need guidance about what to do next after having been immersed in the detailed examination of materials. Include directions on how you would like the reports filed and when the reviewers of the same materials may confer.

Conduct the review. Provide each reviewer with necessary tools, including the *Directions to Reviewers*, their criteria definitions, resource materials, and access to all components of the assigned materials. Reiterate how and when to communicate with other reviewers and how to get questions answered.

Compile the review data for each instructional material. Prepare packets of review results for use in the selection process. First, clip together a packet of all review forms for one piece of instructional material from one reviewer. Then gather all reviews for one piece of instructional material and record the results on the Review Team Summary (Form 6). Staple all Form 5s to the back of Form 6. Forms 5 and 6 will be used throughout the selection process. Label and file the individual reviews; they will be needed from time to time in the selection process.

Resolve any discrepant results. When considering multiple reviewer opinions, it is likely that a few will be quite different from the others. Look back through the detailed reviews and let the evidence cited there make the case. At this point, it is possible to disregard a few reviewer decisions if the reviewer did not make a convincing case; but as a general rule, it is better to include than to exclude.

Summarize the results for use in the selection process. This summary is a bridge from the review step to the selection step. You or a small group should apply judgments, make tentative recommendations, and provide a draft of the Selection Recommendations—Form 7 to help get the selection process started.

To do the ranking, look at one program element at a time, such as fifth grade life science or K-2 investigations. Gather the reviews for all instructional materials that may fulfill that program element (some materials will be considered for more than one element). Taking into consideration the opinions and evidence presented by all reviewers, rank the materials from most promising to least promising. Form 7 provides a format for recording this ranked list, with comments. Examples of comments might be "met 4 of the 5 top standards well, professional development is needed to ensure inquiry standards are met," or "7 standards covered—3 well, 4 incompletely" or "2 of 4 reviewers rated standards achievement 'not at all', content coverage superficial."

Reviewers will not always reach the same conclusions, and may have each made a convincing case for differing conclusions. Carry forward the controversy to the selection process where it can be openly debated and resolved. A carefully designed neutral summary of the reviews will be a helpful addition to the selection recommendations.

This organizing and preliminary ranking will help the launch of "Step 4: Selecting Materials."

Constraints and Cautions

If you have too little time or too few reviewers to handle the number of materials that need to be reviewed, you may need to review the instructional materials by sampling. By confining the review to a sample, you are assuming that the quality of that sample is consistent with the quality of the whole, a risky assumption. If you must sample, choose what to sample with care (i.e., choose the most critical element of study or perhaps the element most in need of improvement in the current program). When sampling, you may want to have reviewers "specialize" in a particular content area or confine their attention to a small set of the standards.

The review process always seems too laborious and lengthy to some reviewers. However, there is simply no substitute for verifying by careful examination that students are likely to achieve the learning goals—the standards—that the teachers and community have agreed are important. At the end of the review process, reviewers state that they understand the science and the science program much better. So, try to keep the reviewers focused on the benefits to the students and to themselves. Provide comfortable accommodations and a lot of positive reinforcement.

If you need to streamline the process, reviewers can review first by one common criterion agreed to be of highest priority. Then a full review can be done only of those materials that passed this initial screening. Applying one screening criterion will work best when there is unanimity among not only reviewers but also the community at large about the attributes of an excellent science curriculum. Rarely is an instructional materials review that clear cut, however. Upon closer examination, some of the discarded materials may have positive attributes that outweigh what were initially perceived to be weaknesses.

DIRECTIONS FOR REVIEWERS

1. Identify the standards for reviewing each unit of instructional materials.

The primary source of information will be the curriculum framework, which identifies the standards to be achieved by students in particular grades or grade ranges. For example, a curriculum framework may indicate that sixth grade students will learn about ecosystems and biological adaptations. The standards that describe in detail what middle grade students should understand and be able to do are then the standards applicable to instructional materials under consideration for use for sixth grade life science or integrated science classes.

When looking at unfamiliar instructional materials, it is not always obvious what standards they address. Consult the overview in the teacher's guide, the table of contents, the index, or sales materials from the publisher for topical references. Typically, this method of surveying will result in a very long list of standards that will not necessarily be achieved by the students, but will simply be mentioned or partially addressed. This problem will be addressed for this review by prioritizing the standards and by the recommended method for review

You may discover that the instructional materials under review meet a student learning goal that was not previously identified, but is represented in the standards. Consult other reviewers of the same materials to determine whether this is a high priority standard, and, if so, reviewers can add it to their lists.

2. Prioritize the standards.

There is probably not enough time to complete a review of all the materials using each identified standard. Therefore, with your facilitator or team, make a prioritized list of the standards you will use. Record all these prioritized standards in the table on Standards Record and Rating Sheet (Form 1). Put the highest priority standards first. Use the identification or numbering system agreed to in the training of reviewers (See "Numbering Standards" in Chapter 5).

3. Get ready to conduct the review.

Gather all the components of the materials you will be reviewing, a copy of the standards, as well as reference books on science literacy, science content for various grade levels, and science teaching. You also should have definitions of the criteria developed during your training.

Now, look through the materials, especially overviews in the teacher's sections and sales materials, the table of contents, any assessment materials, and a list of all the components of the set or unit. "Sticky notes" are convenient for marking sections to which you may return. (You should not write on instructional materials under review, because publishers usually ask for their return in salable condition.)

4. Review what students should understand or be able to do.

Make sure that Form 1 contains your name and the title of the unit or set of instructional materials you are reviewing. Now, read the first or highest priority standard and transfer source, grade, and text information about it to the top of Form 2. Now you will begin to do a review, one standard at a time. As you begin, be sure you understand the science content and level of sophistication implied—what students should understand or be able to do. Do not proceed until this is clear to you and your fellow reviewers. Use the content expertise of the scientists on the team and consult your reference books to develop your understanding of what exactly would constitute achieving each standard.

5. Examine the materials for content coverage and scientific accuracy and importance.

Next, examine in detail the materials to look for content coverage and scien-

tific accuracy and importance. Record what you find and where in detail on Form 2. If it turns out that the content of the standard cannot be found in the materials, record why you think so, and give a "not at all" rating for that standard on Form 4 and in the Summary Rating column for that standard on Form 1. Under these circumstances, there is no point in completing Forms 3 and 5.

6. Determine the likelihood the students will learn content.

When the content of the standard is found in the materials, continue to look through the materials for how well and how often the students are engaged in learning about that content. Look also for how well an average teacher would be supported in planning and carrying out the learning experiences. You will be filling out Form 3, using your own judgment and the definitions of the criteria developed during review training. Provide evidence for your conclusions and cite lessons, section numbers, or text, as appropriate.

If instructional materials do not match any standards, but nevertheless seem worthwhile and well designed, you may be confused. In such cases, reviewers often wonder whether the standards are in error. Although this could be the case, usually it is not, and the materials should not be considered for selection. Topics not found in the standards have usually been intentionally deleted. Also, you may want to refer to standards for other grade levels, since sometimes the topic is found elsewhere and is therefore developmentally inappropriate for the use originally being considered.

Now, make a summary judgment on Form 4 about how likely it is that students would achieve the standard using the unit or set of materials under review. Be sure to give your suggestions for modification or additions as requested. (These will be very helpful in the selection process and for planning professional development if the materials are selected.) Record your rating in the table in Form 1, also. Make notes that will help you complete questions about professional development and essential components in Form 5.

Go back to Form 1 and choose the next standard. Transfer information about that standard to a new set of pages for Forms 2 and 3. Then proceed to judge whether the materials under review contain sufficient amounts of the content in this standard, and so on. When all of the standards listed on Form 1 have been reviewed, complete a summary rating (Form 4).

7. Additional Considerations

On Form 5 you summarize your recommendations for the professional development needed to implement effectively each unit or set of materials you have reviewed. You also identify essential components of the materials needed by the district.

Use a separate Form 5 sheet for each unit or set and be sure to identify at the top which materials you are addressing. When you address professional development, be as specific as possible and apply your knowledge of the level of science background and teaching skills of the "average" teacher. Since you have studied the materials very carefully with student learning in mind, your advice will provide important guidance for those who plan professional development.

Next, you will recommend which components the publisher offers should be purchased, if the materials are selected. Components are parts of the classroom resources that are available separately, such as teacher's guides, student workbooks, videotapes, kits of materials, laser disks, assessment packets, laboratory guides, re-teaching or enrichment materials, and software. List and then rate each, considering its importance to helping students achieve the standards.

What Happens Next?

The facilitator, working with you, will compile a "Review Team Summary" (Form 6), showing how well each reviewed unit or set of instructional materials reflect the prioritized standards. Your judgments recorded on Forms 1-5 will be used in the selection process. Those who ultimately make selection recommendations will use your summary judgments as well as your estimation of the need for professional development and essential components.

STEP 4: SELECTING MATERIALS

To move closer to the goal of making excellent science instructional materials available to students and teachers, the data and judgments collected during review must now be applied to making selections. First, the review data should be compiled and examined. Up to this point, each set of materials was reviewed only against standards. Now, the sets of materials will be compared with one another.

At this time, considerations of cost and professional development likely to be needed for successful implementation are reconciled with resources. Training and supporting the teachers in using the new materials is just as critical to reaching the goal of increased student achievement as choosing good materials.

Finally, another decision-making body, such as a school board, will usually make the final decision about which materials will be purchased. The recommendations developed through the selection process need to make a strong case, citing evidence to support the validity of the process used while focusing on the role of instructional materials in supporting student learning goals.

Recommended Process

Begin the selection process. The review can continue through selection, with the same participants, so that review and selection constitute a seamless process. However, new people will sometimes be involved at this point, due to local decision-making policies or the need to involve other stakeholders, for example. In any case, some review participants should be part of the selection process in order to provide continuity. Any newcomers should be provided with background information about the process so far and engage in a mock review in order to develop understanding of the review data.

Complete the ranking of comparable instructional materials. As described at the end of "Step 3: Reviewing Materials," the selection process begins with examination of a ranked list of instructional materials suitable for a specific grade and content area in the curriculum framework. The recommendations were drafted by the facilitator to help organize the selection process, but should now be examined and revised as necessary. In taking on the selection tasks the participants need to incorporate four elements: (1) review data, (2) information collected in preparing for the review, (3) comparative cost, and (4) professional development requirements.

1. **Review data.** At the end of the review process, the facilitator will have compiled the ratings of all

reviewers for each set of instructional materials using the Review Team Summary (Form 6). These data should be readily available.

It is sometimes necessary to remind participants that it is not the purpose of the selection process to do another review. Refer them instead to the quality of the evidence given by the reviewers to support their ratings. The selection process should respect reviewer decisions, not undo or redo the reviews.

2. **Information collected in preparing for the review.** The preparation step yielded important information about the effectiveness of the current program and the opinions of teachers, administrators, and the community about priorities for improving the science program, as well as policies governing the material review and selection process.

   Note: To save time, apply elements 3 and 4 (below) only to the top-ranked materials—meaning those under serious consideration.

3. **Comparative cost.** Using the Comparative Cost Worksheet, calculate a cost per student for each unit or set of promising materials.

This exercise should reflect reviewer advice on which parts of the program to buy. These costs are negotiable; so publishers should be consulted before making final recommendations.

4. **Professional development requirements.** Consider what resources will be needed to train teachers and provide classroom support for effective use of the most promising materials. Again, the reviewer advice should be taken into account, as well as any available information on the plans of those responsible for future professional development. It is highly desirable for the staff responsible for planning and implementing professional development to be part of this discussion.

For an overview of the selection process see Figure 2.

Fit the most promising instructional materials into the curriculum framework. The most desirable instructional materials for each grade and topical area of the curriculum framework have now been tentatively identified. Put those pieces in place in the framework. The final step of the selection process is studying the proposed overall program, and assuring coherence of the materials at each

Review:
Needs of local program
Goals of selection process
How the review was conducted

Review each Form 7
and make decisions about which materials can be dropped from the selection process. Base these decisions on the review data, without regard to cost or professional development resources likely to be needed.

Prepare a cost/student estimate
for each set of materials. Use Form 8, and reviewers' recommendations on Form 5.

Consider professional development
likely to be needed to implement each set of materials, as noted in reviewers' comments on Form 5.

Make tentative selections
of instructional materials for each subject and grade on Form 7.

Examine the selections
as part of the curriculum framework (relationships across grades and from one grade to another). Consider content, instructional design, and resources likely to be required in implementing each selection.

Negotiate and reconsider
until instructional materials can be recommended for the entire curriculum framework.

FIGURE 2   Selection Process

grade level and across grade spans, while still meeting overall student learning goals. Making final recommendations, particularly for elementary and middle school, entails a great deal of back-and-forth in search of a coherent arrangement, and it may require some adjustments in the original framework to take advantage of the best curriculum materials that are available.

The selection process may fail to identify materials that address content for each grade level. Solutions include continuing to search for materials to put through an ongoing review, writing new materials from scratch, or attempting to fix materials with poor ratings. Constraints and cautions about local efforts to write or fix materials are discussed below.

Complete the selections. Now you have the product of the entire process—recommended instructional materials chosen for their carefully assessed ability to meet student learning goals. Of course, professional development and ongoing materials management are essential for successful implementation. Be sure to specify the recommended components for each selection (software, laser disk, student workbooks, assessment packets, etc.).

Prepare to present a case for approval. The results of planning, training, reviewing, and selecting now must be approved and implemented.

The responsibility of selection participants continues with the requirement to communicate with and persuade decision makers to approve their recommendations. In developing the recommendations report, integrate information about the effectiveness of the current program with how the recommended selections will address related concerns. Point out that the focus of the review was on student learning goals and note any relationships those goals have to current or future achievement tests or graduation requirements. Describe the contacts made with the community and school district administrators, as well as their involvement in the process and any pertinent results or findings. Note the credentials of your reviewers and the extent of their training.

In most localities, an oral presentation will be required—most likely to the school board. Anticipate and prepare to answer questions from school board members, other administrators, and the community. You may want to have summary charts or figures on hand. Have a member of the local scientific community, preferably a member of the review and selection team, speak on behalf of the process and recommendations.

Constraints and Cautions

The selection process may result in recommendations of some instructional materials with lower than desirable ratings. Unfortunately, high-quality instructional materials may not be available for some student learning goals or an unusual sequence or combination of requirements. These important questions should be taken into account:

- Is it possible that appropriate instructional materials do exist, but were not included in the review? Are potentially suitable materials currently under development? If so, could local schools use the materials in a developer's field test?

- Could it be that the topic is inappropriate for the grade level—too sophisticated or too easy for the average developmental level of students? If so, can the curriculum framework be changed?

- If the final result is a mix of materials from various publishers, is the pedagogy consistent across the materials? Will implementation be unduly confusing? Are copyright infringements a possibility?

- If extensive teacher education will be required, are sufficient resources available: release time, leadership, ongoing support, and evaluation?

- If a local team will need to develop an instructional materials unit, are sufficient human resources—both for teaching strategies and scientific subject matter—available? Are there financial resources to support a sufficiently long period of development, field testing, review, revisions, and publication?

- Could a gap in the program remain until suitable instructional materials can be found through a continuing search and mini-review? How long would local policies allow this condition to exist? Are students at risk of failing to pass required tests or meet prerequisites?

For more information on planning and implementing a science program, see *Designing Mathematics or Science Curriculum Programs: A Guide for Using Mathematics and Science Education Standards* (NRC, 1999a) and *Designs for Science Literacy* (AAAS, forthcoming a).

Be prepared to encounter community opposition, particularly if you have not informed and involved the community adequately. A facilitator with strong knowledge of local and state policy, familiarity with applicable standards, and who can show the strengths of the review and selection process should be sufficiently prepared to handle this situation. Try to avoid polarization by listening carefully and acknowledging opposing concerns. Address opposition by providing evidence from the review process and criteria to back up the recommendations.

STEP 5: EVALUATING THE PROCESS AND RESULTS

Developing your local capacity to identify and select instructional materials for the best possible local science program will require several years of effort and ongoing evaluation. As you go through each round of review and selection, lessons learned should be noted and applied to revising the criteria and the processes used. The assumptions and implied goals of the review criteria should be checked against subsequent student achievement and teacher feedback. Having just completed the selection process, you—and participants in the review and selection process—are in a position to recommend ongoing monitoring of the effects and to prepare for the next round. Monitoring may identify the need for supplementation of the choices just made.

Although in many areas the facilitator's job description changes once the science instructional materials are selected—to professional development and implementation concerns or to another subject matter area—continual attention needs to be focused on the efficacy of the new instructional materials. To implement a process of continual improvement, the new program should be monitored in a number of ways, and community involvement should be sustained.

Recommended Process

Gather student achievement data. Review how your district and state will gather data on student achievement with the new materials. The coordination of the implementation of new instructional materials with any new assessment plans, the content of professional development, and knowledge of the political climate will enhance success of the science program (DoEd, 1997a). Analysis of district or state test data, surveys of teachers, and interviews of students can provide evidence of the effectiveness of the materials in helping students achieve the standards.

Also consider more informal opportunities to gather feedback on the science program, such as teacher professional development, meetings of principals, science material distribution centers, a district-wide web site, focus groups, and classroom observations. Keep the focus on standards-based student achievement information, not only to collect convincing data but also to reinforce the message that student achievement is the goal of the science program.

Take another look at the process. If this was not done at the end of the review, reconvene those who were involved in reviewing and selecting the materials to discuss what worked and what did not. Collect their suggestions for future modifications, and with the other key feedback—such as student achievement—begin preparing for the next review and selection round.

The review and selection teams should also discuss their experiences and recommendations with those responsible for professional development, for developing or revising the curriculum framework, and for refurbishing classroom science materials. This kind of internal communication will help develop the capacity to improve the science program continuously.

Continue to strengthen the program. During review and selection, materials may have been recommended that were not highly rated or that were considered incomplete in terms of helping students achieve relevant standards. Identify who will follow through with the suggestions gathered during review and selection. Because new instructional materials are constantly under development, you may want to schedule periodic mini-reviews to identify new materials to replace or supplement those in place.

Continue community involvement. Community interest in the review and selection process should be nurtured and sustained. Be sure that the community is kept aware of—and involved in— the new program in action. Disseminate information gathered in periodic progress reviews. Establish or strengthen a community advisory board. If the community was not wholly supportive of the process or outcome, begin now to involve key community stakeholders in discussions aimed at preparing for the next round of instructional materials selection.

Constraints and Cautions

The demands of implementing the new program may leave no staff or no time to deal with ongoing evaluation and long-term planning. Experience with the information in this guide should help science program administrators articulate their need to collect evidence of program effectiveness continually, develop capacity to understand the role of standards in the science program, keep the community informed, and plan for future reviews of new instructional materials. Resources for evaluation and long-term planning should be given high priority.

If a demand for evidence of student improvement is made in the first year or two, be prepared for student achievement data to be disappointing. Changes in education practice are multidimensional and require numerous changes, such as new teaching approaches and new kinds of materials. All pertinent aspects must change to significantly affect outcome (Fullan, 1991), and that takes time. Gather baseline data and describe reasonable expectations. Explain long-term evaluation plans and methods.

Forms for Use in Review and Selection

Forms 1 through 8 referred to in the preceding section are provided here. Each reviewer will need Forms 1-5 for each instructional material and mutiple copies of Forms 2 and 3. Forms 6-8 are used in the selection process.

To revise or customize these forms, you may wish to begin by copying the form from the website of the National Academy Press <http://www.nap.edu>.

STANDARDS RECORD AND RATING SHEET   FORM 1

Title of Instructional Materials: _____

Name of Reviewer: _____

Use this sheet to record the standards you are using to review the instructional materials, and (after completing Forms 2 and 3) to record how well the materials meet each of those standards. List these standards in order of their priority, with the most important first.

Identify the source(s) for the standards used: _____

_____

	Grade Level	**Identify the Standard** *Write a short version and cite a page number from your standards document.*	**Summary Rating** *(From the end of Form 4).*
1			
2			
3			
4			
5			

Title of Instructional Materials: _____

Name of Reviewer: _____

Use a separate set of Forms 2, 3, and 4 for each standard.

Standard # _____
from Form 1

┌───┐
│ **Provide the complete text of the standard** │
│   │
│   │
│   │
│   │
└───┘

2.1   Is the **content of the standard** found in the materials?
Provide specific evidence, examples, explanations, and references.

2.2 Is the content **scientifically accurate and significant**?
Provide specific evidence, examples, explanations, and references.

Note: *If the content of the materials does not match the standard or is inaccurate or trivial, there is no need to continue the review. Record "not at all" as your summary judgment on Form 4 and in the table on Form 1.*

INSTRUCTIONAL DESIGN REVIEW

FORM 3

Title of Instructional Materials: _____

Name of Reviewer: _____

Standard # _____
from Form 1

```
┌─────────────────────────────────────────────────┐
│                                                   │
│   Provide the complete text of the standard       │
│                                                   │
│                                                   │
│                                                   │
│                                                   │
│                                                   │
└─────────────────────────────────────────────────┘
```

3.1   Do the materials **actively engage** the students to promote their understanding of the subject matter of the standard?
*Consult the definition developed during review training. Provide specific
evidence, examples, explanations, and references. Be sure to consider
whether this material provides all students with the opportunity to be actively
engaged.*

3.2 Will the students develop a **depth of understanding** of the content of the standard through use of the materials?
Consult the definition developed during review training. Provide specific evidence, examples, explanations, and/or references. Be sure to consider whether this material provides all students with the opportunity to develop a depth of understanding.

Note: *SKIP item 3.3 if the standard you are using IS an inquiry standard.*

3.3 Is **scientific inquiry** taught, modeled, and practiced where appropriate? *Consult the definition developed during review training and the inquiry standards. Provide specific evidence, examples, explanations, and references. Be sure to consider whether this material can help all students achieve the standard.*

3.4 Do the materials provide informal and formal **assessments** for both the teacher and student to evaluate progress in achieving the standard?
Provide specific evidence, examples, explanations, and references. Be sure to consider whether the assessments will assist all students in achieving the standard.

SUMMARY RATING

Title of Instructional Materials: _____

Name of Reviewer: _____

Standard # _____ *from Form 1*

Use this sheet to provide your summary rating on how well the materials under review will help all students achieve the standard.

_____ **Completely**

_____ **Almost Completely**
Please comment on modifications or additions needed for the material to meet the standard.

_____ **Incompletely**
Please comment on modifications or additions needed for the material to meet the standard.

_____ **Not at all**

Next steps:
- *Record your summary rating in the right-hand column on Form 1.*
- *Continue your review with the next standard on your list from Form 1. Use a new set of Forms 2, 3, and 4.*
- *When you are finished with all the standards on your list, complete Form 5 to finish your review of these materials.*

ADDITIONAL INFORMATION   FORM 5

Title of Instructional Materials: _____

Name of Reviewer: _____

Complete this after you have completed Forms 2, 3, and 4 with all the standards listed on Form 1.

How much and what kind of **professional development is likely to be needed** by the teachers in order to use these materials effectively?

Most materials are made up of several components (e.g., teacher's manual, materials kit, unit tests, videos, software, enrichment materials). **Which components of the materials under review should be purchased?**

Component	Must have	Optional, high priority	Optional, low priority	Not needed	Not examined

Comments:

REVIEW TEAM SUMMARY

FORM 6

Title of Instructional Materials: _____

Name of Reviewers:

1. _____

2. _____

3. _____

4. _____

To facilitate the selection process, complete a separate team summary for each unit or set of materials reviewed.

Standard	Rating of each reviewer			
	1	2	3	4

For ease in scanning the columns, use these codes:

C = completely

AC = almost completely

I = incompletely

N = not at all

SELECTION RECOMMENDATIONS   FORM 7

Grade Level and Subject: _____
                        (e.g., third grade physical science)

	Title and publisher	**Comments**
1		
2		
3		
4		
5		
6		
7		
8		
9		
10		
11		

COMPARATIVE COST WORKSHEET   FORM 8

Components Needed

Make a combined list of all the components mentioned by reviewers on Form 5 (e.g., teacher's manual, materials kit, unit tests, videos, software, enrichment materials). Then find out the current prices for all the components recommended for selection (for example, the "must have" and "optional, high priority").

Each component should be identified as a "class": either non-consumable (**NC**), completely consumable (**CC**), or a combination (**KIT**), because each is handled separately in estimating cost per student.

Component	Must have	Optional, high priority	Optional, low priority	Not needed	List price	Per	Class (NC, CC or KIT)

Computing Estimated Cost Per Student

Making a reasonable estimate of science material cost requires that you treat the following three categories separately: non-consumable components (textbooks, manuals, videos, software), combinations of consumable and non-consumable items, (kits, sets) and entirely consumable items (student tests, workbooks, chemicals). When materials and equipment are required but are not available from the publisher, you will need to estimate based on the materials list or substitute the cost of a similar package from another publisher.

This estimate is designed to be used for comparative purposes. For actual budget decisions, many more implementation factors need to be taken into consideration. For example, the reuse of a "science kit" implies a refurbishment system that may require new staff and space. Decisions about how to equip a classroom can depend on such teaching practices as cooperative learning or team teaching. Refurbishment costs can be significantly reduced if local bulk ordering eventually replaces buying from the publisher, and so on. The costs for replacing consumable items will also need to cover replacing lost and broken non-consumable items.

Non-consumable (NC) materials   Subtotals

1. List of the non-consumable components and their prices. For each, determine how many are needed to supply one classroom or one period. Multiply the cost by the number needed.

   Add these amounts to get (A) COST OF NC COMPONENTS.   A _____

2. If the materials will be circulated or shared, divide A by the number of times that materials will be used in a year to obtain B.   B _____

3. Divide B by the number of years you expect to use the materials to get (C) COST OF NONCONSUMABLES PER CLASSROOM PER YEAR.   C _____

Combinations containing both consumable and nonconsumable materials (KIT)

4. List the prices of all the KITS used in one classroom in a year. Multiply each unit price by the number needed for each classroom—this is 1 if your class sizes match those provided for by

the supplier. (Large class sizes or teachers who teach more than 1 class perday may require the purchase of more KITS, as well as the purchase of more consumables.) Add all these products to find the Initial Cost of Kits.

D _____

5. Divide D by the estimated number of times each KIT will be refurbished and used in another classroom during one year. Then divide that number by the number of years the KITS will be used. This will give the approximate cost of the non-consumable part of the kits per classroom per year.

E _____

6. Estimate the cost of refurbishing each kit. Mutiply these costs by the number of a particular kit needed per classroom (usually 1). Add all these values to obtain the cost of refurbishment if there is no sharing.

F _____

7. Multiply F by the estimated average number of times each kit will be shared per year. This calculates the value for the total cost of reburbishment per class per year.

G _____

8. Add E and G. This is the Total Cost of Kits Per Classroom Per Year.

H _____

Completely Consumable Components (CC)

9. Determine the number of consumables needed for one class-room or one period during one year. Multiply the cost of each by the number needed. Then add the cost of all consumable components to get (J) COST OF CONSUMABLE COMPO-NENTS PER CLASSROOM PER YEAR.

J _____

Total Cost per Student Per Year

10. Add C, H and J. Divide by the average number of students per classroom or period to get K.

K _____

This is an estimate of the cost per student per year of implementing this set of instructional material.

For more information on buying, refurbishing, and managing science instructional materials, contact the Association of Science Materials Centers listed in "Contact Information."

5
Resources for Training

This chapter contains the training materials, background information, and samples referred to earlier in the report and guide in a format that makes copying these pages convenient. Refer to the Web site of the National Research Council (<http://www.national-academies.org>) for an electronic version of the entire publication (useful for customizing materials). This chapter is composed of the following topics:

Numbering standards

Citing evidence

Defining criteria

"Instructional Analysis" from Project 2061

"Judging How Well Materials Assess Science Learning Goals" from Project 2061

NUMBERING STANDARDS

Numbering the standards assists reviewers in communicating with one another and making written records. If the standards you are using are not numbered, like the *National Science Education Standards* below, adopt a numbering system similar to this example.

It is best to have reviewers write the numbers on their copies of the standards, instead of providing a separate list. Using only a list could encourage a shallow topical review.

SAMPLE FROM THE K-4 SCIENCE CONTENT OF THE *NATIONAL SCIENCE EDUCATION STANDARDS*

A Science as Inquiry (see pp. 121-122)

1 Abilities necessary to do scientific inquiry

a) **Ask a question about objects, organisms, and events in the environment.** This aspect of the standard emphasizes students asking questions that they can answer with scientific knowledge, combined with their own observations. Students should answer their questions by seeking information from reliable sources of scientific information and from their own observations and investigations.

b) **Plan and conduct a simple investigation.** In the earliest years, students may design and conduct simple experiments to answer questions. The idea of a fair test is possible for many students to consider by fourth grade.

> This standard can be referred to as K-4/A1b.

c) **Employ simple equipment and tools to gather data and extend the senses.** In early years, students develop simple skills, such as how to observe, measure, cut, connect, switch, turn on and off, pour, hold, tie, and hook. Beginning with simple instruments, students can use rulers to measure the length, height, and depth of objects and materials; thermometers to measure temperature; watches to measure time; beam balances and spring scales to measure weight and force; magnifiers to observe objects and organisms; and microscopes to observe the finer details of plants, animals, rocks, and other materials. Children also develop skills in the use of computers and calculators for conducting investigations.

B Physical Sciences (pp. 123 and 127)

2 Position and motion of objects

a) The position of an object can be described by locating it relative to another object or the background.

b) An object's motion can be described by tracing and measuring its position over time.

c) The position and motion of objects can be changed by pushing or pulling. The size of the change is related to the strength of the push or pull.

> This standard can be referred to as K-4/B2c.

d) Sound is produced by vibrating objects. The pitch of the sound can be varied by changing the rate of vibration.

CITING EVIDENCE

During review training, examples of good and poor citations for the review criteria provide reviewers with a model and help ensure that convincing evidence is collected. The content criterion (Form 2) is particularly improved by giving examples. The quality and quantity of the evidence becomes important in the selection process (Step 4), and is essential in documenting the rigor of the process. A few examples, shown on overhead transparencies during review training, can be effective in getting the point across. Reviewers also appreciate knowing who may be reading their reviews and why.

Good Examples

- The lessons that highlight the first part of the standard (the Sun can be seen in the daytime) include shadows and model ships, discussion of the shape of the Earth, tracking shadows, the Earth as a sphere, the part of the Earth that is illuminated by the Sun at any one time. (Problem: the models are not necessarily convincing.)
- The lessons do not address why the moon can be seen during the day.
- The "lab" model does reinforce that the Earth rotates. (Problem: it very much reinforces the incorrect notion of a geocentric universe.)
- Missed opportunity. In the Explorations with the Lab there is potential for a full-scale inquiry (e.g., pick a location anywhere in the world, figure out where it is in relation to the equator, and make up a question on how much daylight it has during a particular season).

Fair Examples

- The module covers only the relationship of Sun and Earth, and does not develop a model of the Universe; so the moon and stars are excluded.
- The shadow tracking sheet seems to be an easy and observable way of collecting analyzable data.

Poor Examples

- There are many pieces of content that lend themselves to matching this standard.
- I'm not a teacher—can't respond.

DEFINING CRITERIA

It is critical to the success of the review that definitions of the criteria on Form 3 be agreed upon and understood by all reviewers and be compatible with local needs. To develop a shared understanding of the criteria have the reviewers participate in developing a working definition for each criterion:

- active engagement
- depth of understanding
- scientific inquiry
- assessments

The finished working definitions should be distributed to reviewers with their review forms.

SUGGESTED PROCEDURE

1. Divide the review team into small groups and assign one of the student learning criteria to each group.

2. Each small group should brainstorm, then prioritize, and finally summarize responses to the following questions in brief statements:

   - Why is this criterion important?
   - What are the most important elements for meeting this criterion? Apply your knowledge of effective teaching strategies and research on learning. Consult reference documents on standards and effective science education.
   - What qualities of instructional materials should a reviewer look for in reviewing with this criterion?

3. A representative from each small group can present its products to the others for review and comment. All reviewers need to understand and agree with the definitions of each criterion. If necessary, the small groups should meet again to make revisions.

At this point, you may need to customize the review criterion to meet your needs. It may become apparent that another criterion should be added. Or the group may decide that a certain element of a criterion is so essential it should be made mandatory. This kind of customization is very much in the spirit of this guide and the forms provided. Changes that would compromise the quality of your review would be the deletion of any criterion, the substitution of a scale or checklist for the citing of evidence, or any process that does not focus on one standard at a time.

During development of the tool it was decided that equity concerns can be naturally and appropriately addressed within the four criteria on Form 3. You may want to reexamine your definitions to determine whether the opportunity for all students to learn is adequately addressed. Alternatively, each group could add an equity aspect to each definition, or you could add and define a criterion on addressing diverse learners.

4. The definitions should be distributed with Form 3 during the review.

Suggested resources for the small groups

- Provide copies of the *National Science Education Standards* and *Benchmarks for Science Literacy,* in particular the sections introducing and accompanying the standards, the research citations, and teaching standards.
- The addendum to the *National Science Education Standards* concerning inquiry (NRC, forthcoming) will contain resources to help develop a deeper understanding of scientific inquiry as content subject matter, student abilities, and a teaching strategy.
- Make available the expanded definitions of review criteria from Project 2061's *Identifying Curriculum Materials for Science Literacy: A Project 2061 Evaluation Tool* (Roseman et al., 1997). See "Instructional Analysis." Many applicable terms are defined and described in these comprehensive, thoroughly researched, and field tested criteria.
- The forthcoming *Resources for Science Literacy: Curriculum Materials Evaluation* from AAAS provides complete workshop plans for helping participants understand the meaning of specific learning goals.

- The "guiding principles" in Part II of *In Search of Understanding: The Case for Constructivist Classrooms* (Brooks and Brooks, 1993) may be a useful refresher for those who have studied constructivist learning theories, and may be applicable to the criterion on developing depth of understanding.
- Evaluating the assessments in instructional materials has also been studied and published by staff at Project 2061 (Stern, 1999). These assessment evaluation criteria will be helpful in developing the definitions for assessment criterion 3.4. An excerpt from that paper is in "Judging How Well Materials Assess Science Learning Goals."

INSTRUCTIONAL ANALYSIS
An Excerpt from a Project 2061 Report*

The purpose of the instructional analysis is to estimate how well the material addresses targeted benchmarks from the perspective of what is known about student learning and effective teaching. The criteria for making such judgments are derived from research on learning and teaching and on the craft knowledge of experienced educators. In the context of science literacy, summaries of these have been formulated in Chapter 13: Effective Learning and Teaching in Science for All Americans; in Chapter 15: The Research Base of *Benchmarks for Science Literacy*; and of science education alone in Chapter 3: Science Teaching Standards in *National Science Education Standards*.

From those sources, seven criteria clusters have been identified to serve as a basis for the instructional analysis. (One could view these as standards for instructional materials.) A draft of the specific questions within each cluster is shown below. The proposition here is that (1) in the ideal all questions within each cluster would be well addressed in a material—they are not alternatives; and (2) this analysis has to be made for each benchmark separately—if we are serious about having science literate high school graduates then we want to focus effective instruction on every single one of the important ideas in *Science for All Americans*.

Cluster I, Providing a Sense of Purpose. Part of planning a coherent curriculum involves deciding on its purposes and on what learning experiences will likely contribute to achieving those purposes. But while coherence from the designers' point of view is important, it may be inadequate to give students the same sense of what they are doing and why. This cluster includes criteria to determine whether the material attempts to make its purposes explicit and meaningful, either by itself or by instructions to the teacher.

---

*Excerpt from Roseman, J. E., S. Kesidou, and L. Stern. 1997. *Identifying Curriculum Materials for Science Literacy. A Project 2061 Evaluation Tool*. Based on a paper prepared for the colloquium "Using the *National Science Education Standards* to Guide the Evaluation, Selection, and Adaptation of Instructional Materials." National Research Council, November 10-12, 1996. See <http://project2061.aaas.org/newsinfo/research/roseman/roseman2.html>.

Framing.   Does the material begin with important focus problems, issues, or questions about phenomena that are interesting and/or familiar to students?

Connected sequence.   Does the material involve students in a connected sequence of activities (versus a collection of activities) that build toward understanding of a benchmark(s)?

Fit of frame and sequence.   If there is both a frame and a connected sequence, does the sequence follow well from the frame?

Activity purpose.   Does the material prompt teachers to convey the purpose of each activity and its relationship to the benchmarks? Does each activity encourage each student to think about the purpose of the activity and its relationship to specific learning goals?

Cluster II, Taking Account of Student Ideas.   Fostering better understanding in students requires taking time to attend to the ideas they already have, both ideas that are incorrect and ideas that can serve as a foundation for subsequent learning. Such attention requires that teachers are informed about prerequisite ideas/skills needed for understanding a benchmark and what their students' initial ideas are—in particular, the ideas that may interfere with learning the scientific story. Moreover, teachers can help address students' ideas if they know what is likely to work. This cluster examines whether the material contains specific suggestions for identifying and relating to student ideas.

Prerequisite knowledge/skills.   Does the material specify prerequisite knowledge/skills that are necessary to the learning of the benchmark(s)?

Alerting to commonly held ideas.   Does the material alert teachers to commonly held student ideas (both troublesome and helpful) such as those described in *Benchmarks* Chapter 15: The Research Base?

Assisting the teacher in identifying students' ideas.   Does the material include suggestions for teachers to find out what their students think about familiar phenomena related to a benchmark before the scientific ideas are introduced?

Addressing commonly held ideas. Does the material explicitly address commonly held student ideas?

Assisting the teacher in addressing identified students' ideas. Does the material include suggestions for teachers on how to address ideas that their students hold?

Cluster III, Engaging Students with Phenomena. Much of the point of science is explaining phenomena in terms of a small number of principles or ideas. For students to appreciate this explanatory power, they need to have a sense of the range of phenomena that science can explain. "Students need to get acquainted with the things around them—including devices, organisms, materials, shapes, and numbers—and to observe them, collect them, handle them, describe them, become puzzled by them, ask questions about them, argue about them, and then try to find answers to their questions." (SFAA, p. 201) Furthermore, students should see that the need to explain comes up in a variety of contexts.

First-hand experiences. Does the material include activities that provide first-hand experiences with phenomena relevant to the benchmark when practical and when not practical, make use of videos, pictures, models, simulations, etc.?

Variety of contexts. Does the material promote experiences in multiple, different contexts so as to support the formation of generalizations?

Questions before answers. Does the material link problems or questions about phenomena to solutions or ideas?

Cluster IV, Developing and Using Scientific Ideas. *Science for All Americans* includes in its definition of science literacy a number of important yet quite abstract ideas—e.g., atomic structure, natural selection, modifiability of science, interacting systems, common laws of motion for earth and heavens. Such ideas cannot be inferred directly from phenomena, and the ideas themselves were developed over many hundreds of years as a result of considerable discussion and debate about the cogency of theory and its relationship to collected evidence.

Science literacy requires that students see the link between phenomena and ideas and see the ideas themselves as useful. This cluster includes criteria to determine whether the material attempts to provide links between phenomena and ideas and to demonstrate the usefulness of the ideas in varied contexts.

Building a case. Does the material suggest ways to help students draw from their experiences with phenomena, readings, activities, etc., to develop an evidence-based argument for benchmark ideas? (This could include reading material that develops a case.)

Introducing terms. Does the material introduce technical terms only in conjunction with experience with the idea or process and only as needed to facilitate thinking and promote effective communication?

Representing ideas. Does the material include appropriate representations of scientific ideas?

Connecting ideas. Does the material explicitly draw attention to appropriate connections among benchmark ideas (e.g., to a concrete example or instance of a principle or generalization, to an analogous idea, or to an idea that shows up in another field)?

Demonstrating/modeling skills and use of knowledge. Does the material demonstrate/model or include suggestions for teachers on how to demonstrate/model skills or the use of knowledge?

Practice. Does the material provide tasks/questions for students to practice skills or using knowledge in a variety of situations?

Cluster V, Promoting Student Reflection. No matter how clearly materials may present ideas, students (like all people) will make their own meaning out of it. Constructing meaning well is facilitated by having students (a) make their ideas and reasoning explicit, (b) hold them up to scrutiny, and (c) recast them as needed. This cluster includes criteria for whether the material suggests how to help students express, think about, and reshape their ideas to make better sense of the world.

Expressing ideas. Does the material routinely include suggestions (such as group work or journal writing) for having each student express, clarify, justify, and represent his/her ideas? Are suggestions made for when and how students will get feedback from peers and the teacher?

Reflecting on activities. Does the material include tasks and/or question sequences to guide student interpretation and reasoning about phenomena and activities?

Reflecting on when to use knowledge and skills. Does the material help or include suggestions on how to help students know when to use knowledge and skills in new situations?

Self-monitoring. Does the material suggest ways to have students check their own progress and consider how their ideas have changed and why?

Cluster VI, Assessing Progress. There are several important reasons for monitoring student progress toward specific learning goals. Having a collection of alternatives can ease the creative burden on teachers and increase the time available to analyze student responses and make adjustments in instruction based on them. This cluster includes criteria for whether the material includes a variety of goal-relevant assessments.

Alignment to goals. Assuming a content match of the curriculum material to this benchmark, are assessment items included that match the content?

Application. Does the material include assessment tasks that require application of ideas and avoid allowing students a trivial way out, like using a formula or repeating a memorized term without understanding?

Embedded. Are some assessments embedded in the curriculum along the way, with advice to teachers as to how they might use the results to choose or modify activities?

Cluster VII, Enhancing the Learning Environment. Many other important considerations are involved in the selection of curriculum materials—for example, the help they provide teachers in encouraging student curiosity and creating a classroom community where all can succeed, or the material's scientific accuracy or attractiveness. Each of these can influence student learning, even whether the materials are used. The criteria listed in this cluster provide reviewers with the opportunity to comment on these and other important features.

Teacher content learning. Would the material help teachers improve their understanding of science, mathematics, and technology and their interconnections?

Classroom environment. Does the material help teachers to create a classroom environment that welcomes student curiosity, rewards creativity, encourages a spirit of healthy questioning, and avoids dogmatism?

Welcoming all students. Does the material help teachers to create a classroom community that encourages high expectations for all students, that enables all students to experience success, and that provides all different kinds of students a feeling of belonging to the science classroom?

Connecting beyond the unit. Does the material explicitly draw attention to appropriate connections to ideas in other units?

Other strengths. What, if any, other features of the material are worth noting?

JUDGING HOW WELL MATERIALS ASSESS SCIENCE LEARNING GOALS
An Excerpt from a Project 2061 Report*

CRITERION 1. ALIGNING TO GOALS. Assuming a content match between the curriculum material and the benchmark, are assessment items included that match the same benchmark?

Indicators of meeting the criterion:

1. The specific ideas in the benchmark are **necessary** in order to respond to the assessment items.

2. The specific ideas in the benchmark are **sufficient** to respond to the assessment items (or, if other ideas are needed, they are not more sophisticated and have been taught earlier).

CRITERION 2. TESTING FOR UNDERSTANDING. Does the material assess understanding of benchmark ideas and avoid allowing students a trivial way out, like repeating a memorized term or phrase from the text without understanding?

Indicators of meeting the criterion:

1. Assessment items focus on **understanding** of benchmark ideas (as opposed to recall).

2. Assessment items include both **familiar and novel** tasks.

CRITERION 3. INFORMING INSTRUCTION. Are some assessments embedded in the curriculum along the way, with advice to teachers as to how they might use the results to choose or modify activities?

---

*Stern, L. 1999. *Are you really testing for science literacy? Aiming precisely at benchmarks and standards.* Paper presented at the annual meeting of the National Association for Research in Science Teaching, Boston, Mass., March 28-31.

Indicators of meeting the criterion.

1.   The material uses embedded assessment as a **routine strategy** (rather than just including occasional questions).

2.   The material suggests how to **probe beyond students' initial responses** to clarify and further understand student answers.

3.   The material provides **specific suggestions** to teachers about how to use the information from the embedded assessments **to make instructional decisions** about what ideas need to be addressed by further activities.

Contact Information

The National Research Council's (NRC) publications, including this report, are available on the World Wide Web at <http://www.nap.edu>. Inquiries to the NRC's Center for Science, Mathematics, and Engineering Education can be sent by electronic mail to <csmeeinq@nas.edu>.

The National Science Resources Center, collects and disseminates information about exemplary teaching resources, develops and disseminates curriculum materials, and sponsors outreach activities, specifically in the areas of leadership development and technical assistance, to help school districts develop and sustain hands-on science programs. More information is available at <http://www.si.edu/nsrc>.

The Association of Science Materials Centers (ASMC) offers assistance in planning facilities, identifying and evaluating curriculum, procuring and managing materials, staffing, raising and managing funds, planning a delivery system, developing community support, providing for continuous professional development, and promoting systemic change. ASMC information is available at <http://substorm.astro.umd.edu/ ~asmc/asmc.html>.

The American Association for the Advancement of Science's Project 2061 makes its many resources and research publications available at <http:// project2061.aaas.org>.

References

AAAS (American Association for the Advancement of Science). 1989. *Science for All Americans.* New York: Oxford University Press. Internet address: http://project2061.aaas.org/tools/sfaaol/sfaatoc.htm

AAAS. 1993. *Benchmarks for Science Literacy.* New York: Oxford University Press. Internet address: http://project2061.aaas.org/tools/benchol/bolframe.html

AAAS. 1997. *Resources for Science Literacy: Professional Development.* New York: Oxford University Press. Internet address: http://project2061.aaas.org/tools/rsl/index.html

AAAS. Forthcoming [a]. *Designs for Science Literacy.* Internet address: http://project2061.aaas.org/tools/designs/index.html

AAAS. Forthcoming [b]. *Middle Grades Science Textbooks: A Benchmarks-based Evaluation.*

AAAS. Forthcoming [c]. *Resources for Science Literacy: Curriculum Materials Evaluation.* Internet address: http://project2061.aaas.org/tools/rslcme/index.html

Brearton, M. A., and S. Shuttleworth. 1999. Racing a comet. *Journal of Staff Development* winter:30-33. Internet address: http://project2061.aaas.org/newsinfo/research/articles/nsdc_jsd.htm

Brooks, J. G., and M. G. Brooks. 1993. *In Search of Understanding: The Case for Constructivist Classrooms.* Alexandria, Va: Association for Supervision and Curriculum Development.

Bush, W. S., G. Kulm, and D. Surati. Forthcoming. *Preparing teachers for mathematics textbook selection.*

Bybee, R. W. Ed. 1996. *National Standards and the Science Curriculum: Challenges, Opportunities and Recommendations.* Dubuque, Iowa: Kendall/Hunt.

Bybee, R. W. 1997. *Achieving Scientific Literacy: From Purposes to Practices.* N. H.: Heinemann.

CBEDS (California Basic Educational Data System). 1997. *California Public School Enrollment.* Sacramento: Educational Demographics Unit, California Department of Education.

CCSSO (Council of Chief State School Officers). 1997. *Mathematics and science content standards and curriculum frameworks: States' progress on development and implementation.* Internet address: http://www.ccsso.org

Celebuski, C. 1998. *Status of Education Reform in Public Elementary and Secondary Schools: Principal's Perspective.* Washington, D.C.: U.S. Department of Education.

Chubb, J. 1999. Interview about the Edison Project with its director of curriculum and assessment, March 10, 1999.

CPRE (Consortium for Policy Research in Education). 1996. *Tracking student achievement in science and math: The promise of state assessment programs.* Policy brief RB-17-July 1996, pp. 4-5. Internet address: http://www.upenn.edu/gse/cpre/frames/pubs.html

DoEd (U.S. Department of Education). 1997a. *Assessment of student performance: Studies of education reform.* Internet address: http://www.ed.gov/pubs/SER/ASP/

DoEd. 1997b. *Attaining Excellence: Guidebook to Examine School Curricula.* Washington, D.C.: Office of Educational Research and Improvement.

DoEd.1997c. *Guidelines for Submitting Science Programs for Review.* Washington, D.C.: Office of Educational Research and Improvement.

Fullan, M. 1991. *The New Meaning of Educational Change.* New York: Teachers College Press.

Hutchinson, J., and M. Huberman. 1993. *Knowledge dissemination and use in science and mathematics education: A literature review.* Prepared for the Directorate of Education and Human Resources, Division of Research, Evaluation and Dissemination, National Science Foundation by The Network. Document nsf9375. Internet address:: http://www.nsf.gov/cgi-bin/getpub?nsf9375

IMF (Instructional Materials Fund). 1989. Policy (K-8), California Education Code Section 60242(b) (1989, amd.1998).

James, C. 1999. Interview with former science teacher, Saint Patrick's Episcopal Day School, Washington, D.C., March 1999.

Kesidou, S. 1999. Producing analytical reports on curriculum materials in science: Findings from Project 2061's 1998 curriculum review study. Paper presented at the annual meeting of the National Association for Research in Science Teaching. Boston, Mass., March 28-31.

Kulm, G, and L. Grier. 1998. Mathematics curriculum materials reliability study. Washington, D.C.: Project 2061, American Association for the Advancement of Science.

Lee, O., D. C. Eichinger, C. W. Anderson, G. D. Berkheimer, and T. S. Blakeslee. 1993. Changing middle school students' conceptions of matter and molecules. *Journal of Research in Science Teaching* 30:249-70.

Little, J. W. 1993. *Teachers' Professional Development and Education Reform.* CPRE Policy Brief No. RB-11-10/93, pp. 1-7. Internet address: http://www.upenn.edu/gse/cpre/frames/pubs.html

Loucks-Horsley, S., K. Stiles, and P. Hewson. 1996. *Principles of Effective Professional Development for Mathematics and Science Education.* NISE Policy Briefs, vol 1, no. 1. Madison, Wisc.: National Institute for Science Education. Internet address: http://www.wcer.wisc.edu/nise/Publications/Briefs/default.html

McArthur Parker, C. 1999. Interview with chemistry teacher, Edmund Burke School, Washington, D.C., March 1999.

Massell, D., M. Kirst, and M. Hoppe. 1997. *Persistence and Change: Standards-based Systemic Reform in Nine States.* Consortium for Policy Research in Education Policy Brief No. RB-21-March 1997. Internet address: http://www.upenn.edu/gse/cpre/frames/pubs.html

NCEE (National Commission of Excellence in Education). 1983. *A Nation at Risk: The Imperative for Educational Reform.* Washington, D.C.: U.S. Government Printing Office.

NCES (National Center for Education Statistics). 1998a. *Facing the Consequences: Using TIMSS for a Closer Look at United States Mathematics and Science Education.* London: Kluwer Academic.

NCES. 1998b. *NAEP 1996 Science Cross-state Data Compendium for the Grade 8 Assessment.* Washington, D.C.: U.S. Government Printing Office.

NEGP (National Education Goals Panel). 1998. *Mathematics and Science Achievement State by State (1998).* Washington, D.C: U.S. Government Printing Office.

NAS (National Academy of Sciences). 1998. *Teaching About Evolution and the Nature of Science.* Washington, D.C.: National Academy Press. Internet address: http://books.nap.edu/catalog/5787.html

NRC (National Research Council). 1996. *National Science Education Standards.* Washington, D.C.: National Academy Press. Internet address: http://books.nap.edu/catalog/4962.html

NRC. 1997a. *Introducing the National Science Education Standards.* Washington, D.C.: National Academy Press. Internet address: http://books.nap.edu/catalog/5704.html

NRC. 1997b. *Science Teacher Preparation in an Era of Standards-based Reform.* Washington, D.C.: National Academy Press. Internet address: http://books.nap.edu/catalog/9078.html

NRC. 1998. *Every Child a Scientist: Achieving Scientific Literacy for All.* Washington, D.C.: National Academy Press. Internet address: http://books.nap.edu/catalog/6005.html

NRC. 1999a. *Designing Mathematics or Science Curriculum Programs: A Guide for Using Mathematics and Science Education Standards.* Washington, D.C.: National Academy Press.

NRC. 1999b. *How People Learn: Brain, Mind, Experience, and School.* Washington, D.C.: National Academy Press. Internet address: http://www.nap.edu/catalog/6160.html

NRC. Forthcoming. *Inquiry and the National Science Education Standards.* Washington, D.C.: National Academy Press.

NSB (National Science Board). 1998. *Failing Our Children: Implications of the Third International Mathematics and Science Study.* Arlington, Va.: National Science Foundation.

Internet address: http://www.nsf.gov/nsb/
documents/1998/nsb98154/nsb98154.htm

NSB. 1999. *Preparing our Children: Math and Science Education in the National Interest.* Arlington, Va.: National Science Foundation. Internet address: http://www.nsf.gov/nsb/documents/1999/nsb9931/nsb9931.htm

NSF (National Science Foundation). 1997. *Review of Instructional Materials for Middle School Science.* Document number NSF 97 54. Washington, D.C.: Directorate for Education and Human Resources, Division of Elementary, Secondary and Informal Education. Internet address: http://www.nsf.gov/pubs/1997/nsf9754/nsf9754.htm>.

NSRC (National Science Resources Center). 1988. *Science for Children: Resources for Teachers.* Washington, D.C.: National Academy Press.

NSRC. 1996. *Resources for Teaching Elementary School Science.* Washington, D.C.: National Academy Press. Internet address: http://books.nap.edu/catalog/4966.html

NSRC. 1998. *Resources for Teaching Middle School Science.* Washington, D.C.: National Academy Press. Internet address: http://books.nap.edu/catalog/5774.html

Ohio Systemic Initiative. 1998. *The NSES-based Inventory of Middle Level Science Curriculum Study.* Internet address: http://www.discovery.k12.oh.us/nses/nses.html>

Orpwood, G. 1998. The logic of advice and deliberation: Making sense of science curriculum talk. In *Problems of Meaning in Science Curriculum*, eds., D. A. Roberts and L. Östman, pp. 133-49. New York: Teachers College Press.

Roseman, J. E. 1997a. Lessons from Project 2061: Practical ways to implement benchmarks and standards. *The Science Teacher* 64(1):26-29. Internet address: http://project2061.aaas.org/newsinfo/research/roseman/roseman1.html

Roseman, J. E. 1997b. The Project 2061 curriculum-analysis procedure. In *Attaining Excellence: Guidebook to Examine School Curricula*, ed. M. E. McNeely, pp. 125-40. Washington, D.C.: U.S. Department of Education. Internet address: http://project2061.aaas.org/newsinfo/research/enc/enctims.htm

Roseman, J. E., S. Kesidou, and L. Stern. 1997. Identifying curriculum materials for science literacy: A Project 2061 evaluation tool. Paper presented at the NRC colloquium "Using the National Science Education Standards to Guide the Evaluation, Selection, and Adaptation of Instructional Materials." Washington, D.C. November 1996. Internet address: http://project2061.aaas.org/newsinfo/research/roseman/roseman2.html

Rotberg, I. C. 1998. Interpretation of International Test Score Comparisons. *Science* 280:1030-31.

Schmidt, W. H., and C. C. McKnight. 1998. What can we really learn from TIMMS? *Science* 282:1830-31.

Schmidt, W. H., C. C. McKnight, and S. A. Raizen. 1997. *A Splintered Vision: An Investigation of U.S. Science and Mathematics Education.* Boston: Kluwer Academic. Executive summary available on the Internet: http://ustimss.msu.edu/splintrd.htm

Stedman, J. B. 1993 (and update reports). *Goals 2000: Educate America Act, Overview and Analysis.* Washington, D.C.: Congressional Research Service, Library of Congress.

Stern, L. 1999. Are you really testing for science literacy? Aiming precisely at benchmarks and standards. Paper presented at the annual meeting of the National Association for Research in Science Teaching, Boston, Mass., March 28-31.

Tyson, H. 1997. Overcoming structural barriers to good textbooks. Paper prepared for and available from the National Education Goals Panel. Internet address: http://www.negp.gov/Reports/tyson.htm

Tyson-Bernstein, H. 1988. *America's Textbook Fiasco: A Conspiracy of Good Intentions.* Washington, D.C.: Council for Basic Education.

Webb, N. L. 1997. *Determining Alignment of Expectations and Assessments in Mathematics and Science Education.* National Institute for Science Education, Brief Vol. 1, No. 2, January 1997. Internet address: http://www.wcer.wisc.edu/NISE/

Weiss, I. R. 1991. *Curricular Materials for Mathematics and Science: Usage and Perceived Needs From the Field.* Chapel Hill, N.C: Horizon Research.

Wheeler, G. 1999a. Information reported on a 1996 survey of members of the National Science Teachers Association (NSTA) by the NSTA Office of Public Information.

Wheeler, G. 1999b. Information reported from the National Science Teachers Association's general registry.

Woodward, A., and D. L. Elliott. 1990. Textbooks: Consensus and controversy. In *Textbooks and Schooling in the United States: Eighty-ninth Yearbook of the National Society for the Study of Education, Part I.* Chicago: University of Chicago Press.

Index

A

Accuracy, content, 7, 13, 14, 18, 20, 27, 34, 42, 57, 62, 106

Achievement, *see* Student achievement

Activity-based learning, *see* Experiments, laboratory; Research-based teaching

Additional Information (Form 5), 85-86
use of, 62, 63, 67

Administrators, 4, 11, 29, 41, 44, 57, 65, 71

Age factors, 6

American Association for the Advancement of Science, 4, 100
Project 2061, 17-18, 25, 48, 49, 95, 100, 101, 102-109
see also Benchmarks for Science Literacy

Association of Science Materials Centers, 111

Awards and prizes, 7-9

B

Benchmarks for Science Literacy, 3, 4, 5, 7, 48, 49, 52, 56, 100, 102
Project 2061, 18
prototype evaluation, 25, 26, 28, 35

Bias, 48

Budgetary issues, 10, 13, 25, 28, 31, 35, 43, 44-45, 48, 49, 55, 65, 66, 67, 91-93

C

California, 5, 9

CD-ROMs, 58, 63

Center for Science, Mathematics, and Engineering Education, 6, 21-22, 37

Checklists, 24, 26, 43

Committees for materials selection, 11-12, 13, 43, 46-48, 57-58, 99-100
bias, 48
NSF guidelines, 20
Project 2061, 18, 48
prototype evaluation, 24, 28-35, 36, 48
recruitment of, 46-48
scientists on, 26-27, 32, 33, 44-45, 46, 47, 57, 68
training of evaluators, 31-36, 43-49, 51-56, 57

Community involvement, 6, 25-26, 46, 49, 57, 65, 70, 71
political factors, 9, 28, 48

Comparative Cost Worksheet (Form 8), 91-93
use of, 67

Content issues, 7, 24, 26, 43, 50, 51-52, 57
accuracy, 7, 13, 14, 18, 20, 27, 34, 42, 57, 62, 106
checklists, 24, 26, 43
form for evaluation (Forms 2 and 3), 62-63, 77-78, 80, 98
NSF, 20
process flowchart, 54
Project 2061, 18
prototype evaluation, 27, 33
see also Curriculum design and implementation; Textbooks

Content Review (Form 2), 77-78
    use of, 62, 63
Copyright, 69
Cost factors, 10, 13, 25, 28, 31, 35, 43, 44-45, 48,
        49, 55, 65, 66, 67, 91-93 (Form 8)
Council of Chief State Officers, 9
Curriculum design and implementation, overall,
        5, 6, 12, 14, 42, 65, 67, 106
    CMSEE, 21
    NSF, 20
    NSRC, 19
    Project 2061, 17, 48, 102
    prototypes, 25, 27
    reviewer training, 43, 45, 49, 51
    textbooks *vs*, 7
Curriculum framework, 42, 61, 66, 67

D

Demographic factors, 6, 46
Department of Education, 20-21
*Designing Mathematics or Science Curriculum
        Programs: A Guide for Using Mathematics
        and Science Education Standards*, 21, 43, 69
Designs for Science Literacy, 43, 69
Directions to reviewers, 59, 61-64
District of Columbia, 4-5

E

Economic factors
    materials selection and purchasing budgets,
        10, 13, 25, 28, 31, 35, 43, 44-45, 48, 49, 55,
        65, 66, 67, 91-93
    math and science education, importance of, 3-
        4
Edison Project, 11
Enrollment data, 46
Equipment, laboratory, 5, 96-97
Equity, 100

Evaluation, general, 11, 14-15, 19-20, 23-38, 43
    CMSEE, 21-22
    data collection, 45-46, 51, 59, 66, 70, 71
    Department of Education, 20-21
    field testing, 23, 24, 28-37
    forms used in material review,
        copies of, 73-93
        use of, 59, 61, 62-63, 66, 67
    principles of, 23, 25-28
    process, 39-71
        flowcharts, 54, 67
    Project 2061, 17-18, 48
    prototypes, 23, 25-29, 48
    sampling procedures, 60
    training of evaluators, 31-36, 43-49, 51-59
    see also Committees for materials selection;
        Standards-based approach; Testing
*Evaluation Criteria for Science Curriculum
        Materials*, 25
Evolution, 22
Experiments, laboratory, 5, 6, 12, 13, 52, 96

F

Federal government, 3, 4
Field testing, 23, 24, 28-37
Florida, 9
Forms used in material review
    copies of, 73-93
    use of, 59, 61, 62-63, 66, 67, 98-99

G

Gender factors, 46

H

History of science, 12
How People Learn, 35

Principals, *see* Administrators
Private schools, 11-12
Probeware, 58
Professional development
    evaluator training, 31-36, 43-49, 51-59
    form for rating (Form 5), 63-64, 67, 85
    teachers, 6, 10, 13-14, 18, 24, 27-28, 35, 43-48,
        52, 53, 54, 59, 63-70, 85
Project 2061, 17-18, 25, 95, 100, 101-109
Prototypes, 23, 25-29, 48
    Benchmarks, 25, 26, 28, 35
    National Science Education Standards, 25, 26,
        28, 35
    state-level issues, 26, 27, 29, 33
    see also Field testing
Public schools, 9-11
Publishing industry, role of, 10, 11, 12, 47, 49-50,
    58, 62, 69

R

Racial/ethnic factors, 46
Reading level considerations, 12
Reference materials, 52-53
Research-based teaching, 6, 18, 35, 38
*Resources for Science Literacy: Curriculum
    Materials Evaluation*, 100
Resources for Teaching Elementary School Science,
    19
Review Team Summary (Form 6), 87
    use of, 63, 66
Rote learning, *see* Memorization

S

Sampling, 60
School districts, 3, 4, 6, 13, 51, 57
    materials selection procedures, 9-11, 15, 23,
        26, 27, 28, 44, 65, 89
    prototype evaluation, 27, 28
    standards, 10, 11, 32, 42

Science and Technology for Children, 19
Science for All Americans, 102, 104
Scientists as material reviewers, 26-27, 32, 33, 44-
    45, 46, 47, 57, 68
Selection Recommendations (Form 7), 89
    use of, 67
Social factors, 3-4, 37
    community involvement, 6, 25-26, 46, 49, 57,
        65, 70, 71
    NSF guidelines, 20
    parental involvement, 6, 8, 14, 45-46
    political factors, 9, 28, 48
Software, 58
*A Splintered Vision: An Investigation of U.S.
    Science and Mathematics Education*, 9
Stakeholders, *see* Community involvement;
    Parental involvement; Political factors;
    Social factors
Standards-based approach, 3-16, 25-29, 42, 45,
    57-61, 71
    community understanding of, 46
    Edison Project, 11
    forms for reviewers, 53, 61, 62, 63, 75-85
    inquiry-based teaching, 14
    prioritizing, 61, 63-64, 96-97, 99
    process flowcharts, 54, 67
    publishers, 12, 49-50
    reviewer training, 31-37, 43, 44, 46, 47-48, 51-
        56
    school districts, 10, 11, 32, 42
    selection committees use of, 10
    state, 9, 15, 26, 32, 48, 69
    summary ratings, 85, 87
    see also Benchmarks for Science Literacy;
        Content issues; *National Science Education
        Standards*; National standards
Standards Record and Rating Sheet (Form 1), 75
    use of, 61, 62, 63
State-level factors, 3, 4-5, 6, 8
    materials selection procedures, 9-10, 41, 44, 69
    political factors, 9
    prototype evaluation, 26, 27, 29, 33
    standards, 9, 15, 26, 32, 48, 69

Student achievement, 8, 34, 42, 45, 46, 49, 51, 59, 60, 63, 65, 70-71
  see also Standards-based approach; Testing
Summary Rating (Form 4), 83
  use of 62, 63
Summary ratings, 18, 34, 43, 45, 52, 53, 54, 57, 59
  forms, 57, 85, 87

T

Teachers, 5, 15, 27, 42-43
  innovative materials, 13
  manuals and guides for, 14, 52, 57-58, 63, 86
  NSF guidelines, 19, 20
  PAEMST teachers, 7-8
  professional development, 6, 10, 13-14, 18, 24, 27-28, 35, 43-48, 52, 53, 54, 59, 63-70, 85
  Project 2061, 18
  support for, general, 5, 6, 62, 104, 107, 111
  surveys of materials currently used, 45, 70
  textbook use, 7-8, 12, 13
Teaching About Evolution and the Nature of Science, 22
Teams, reviewers, *see* Committees for materials selection
Testing
  classroom assessments, 8
  multiple-choice formats, 8
  PAEMST teachers, 7-8
  professional development in, 46
  statewide, 8
  TIMSS, 4, 7

Texas, 9
Textbooks, 4, 5, 12, 13, 33
  parental involvement, 8
  private schools, 11-12
  state selection procedures, 9
  teacher lesson plans and, 7-8, 12, 13
Third International Mathematics and Science Study, 4, 7

U

University resources, 12, 46, 47

V

Videotapes, 58, 63

W

Washington, D.C., 4-5
World Wide Web, *see* Internet